RALLY
CO-DRIVING

Patrick Stephens Limited, a member of the Haynes Publishing Group, has published authoritative, quality books for enthusiasts for a quarter of a century. During that time the company has established a reputation as one of the world's leading publishers of books on aviation, maritime, military, model-making, motor cycling, motoring, motor racing, railway and railway modelling subjects. Readers or authors with suggestions for books they would like to see published are invited to write to: The Editorial Director, Patrick Stephens Limited, Sparkford, Nr Yeovil, Somerset, BA22 7JJ.

RALLY
CO-DRIVING

A champion's guide to the way to the top

PHIL SHORT

Patrick Stephens Limited

First published in 1992

British Library Cataloguing in Publication Data:
A catalogue record for this book is available from the British
Library

ISBN 1 85260 435 2

Patrick Stephens Limited is a member of the Haynes Publishing
Group P.L.C., Sparkford, Nr Yeovil, Somerset, BA22 7JJ.

Printed in Great Britain by The Bath Press, Bath, Avon.

Contents

Part 3

CULTURED CO-DRIVING   **173**

Foreword

In my early days as a rally driver I heard the phrase, 'A co-driver cannot win rallies—he can only lose them for a driver'. Phil Short is one exception to that rule. His experience and knowledge have helped me to many successes during our six year partnership, one of the longest in the British Open Championship's history.

Our relationship began in 1985 when I started my professional career with Audi Sport UK and over the years Phil has imparted to me his wealth of experience and his professional approach to everything he does, assisting me to two Open Championships, a good run on the European Championship and many International wins, so that I was able to move on to

David Llewellin—British Open Rally Champion Driver, 1989 and 1990. (Lodge.)

World Championship rallying. We even achieved a rarity these days—a British crew leading the RAC Rally!

In the time we spent together I learned the importance of team effort and came to admire Phil's ability to unite the whole team and produce the best possible results from everyone involved. He is also well respected by manufacturer teams, sponsors, administrators, event organizers and marshals, without any of whom the sport of rallying would not exist.

His experience, wisdom and occasionally dry sense of humour make him the ideal author for a book on co-driving, and I am sure that all of you who read this book—co-drivers, drivers or whoever—will, like me, learn much from the British Co-driving Legend.

David Llewellin,
British Open Champion Driver, 1989 and 1990

Acknowledgements

I would like to thank Graham Robson for his encouragement and advice, without which I might never have even started to write this book. Graham also kindly agreed to read through the final offering, as did Tim Tennant and Steve Bond, whom I thank most sincerely for their contributions on Club, National and International co-driving, in addition to several other people within the sport who made helpful suggestions. My wife Lyn carried out innumerable secretarial and administrative tasks, as well as providing me with moral support as the book took shape.

In addition to my principal photographers, Gavin Lodge and Les Kolczak, I would also like to thank Norman Hodson of *Cars and Car Conversions*, Martin Holmes and Maurice Selden for their particular photographs. My son, Andrew Short, took the studio photographs with the help of Gavin Lodge.

The maps in this book are reproduced from the Ordnance Survey maps with the permission of the Controller of HMSO, © Crown Copyright.

Finally, I would like to thank David Llewellin, not only for his kind words in the Foreword, but also for putting up with me as his co-driver for six years, through thick and thin. Indeed, I must thank all my drivers over 25 years of co-driving, the well-known and the little-known, without whom I could never have gained the experience upon which this book is founded. Thank you all, it was a great pleasure and privilege.

Introduction

The sport of rallying has enjoyed several decades of success and popularity. This has been due to prolonged involvement by motor manufacturers, who rightly see it as a promotional vehicle for their products. Unlike Formula One, for instance, rally cars are closely related to the everyday cars the general public buys and drives, hence the connection from a marketing point of view. Few other sports provide a competition primarily for commercially available products—there's no sport for washing machines or cans of beans or pullovers, for example. The other attraction is the widely varying terrain, from tarmac to gravel to snow and ice, often in beautiful and spectacular scenery, rather than the somewhat artificial amphitheatre of a motor racing circuit. The appeal is in the battle of men and machine against the elements, sometimes over treacherous roads or in appalling weather conditions. Thanks to television, the finer points of rallying have come to be appreciated by many more people in recent years, yet this way of viewing the sport does not prevent hundreds of thousands trekking out to remote places to see the action at close quarters; rallying is a sport where the public can see and meet the stars as they travel the country of an event.

While the sport has changed in many ways, there have always been (at least) two people in a rally car, the second person to carry out a number of functions. That person used to be called (and sometimes still is) the navigator, though the term 'co-driver' (itself a bit of a misnomer) is the more usual nowadays. Until the regular use of the in-car camera, few people outside a rally car realized the contribution a good co-driver could make. The co-driver was a make-weight, there because the rules said he had to be and sometimes referred to disparagingly as the 'sack of spuds'. In certain circumstances, a driver might indeed get away with a 'sack of spuds' alongside him, but under the pressure of real competition, a good co-driver is worth far more than his weight, in terms of planning, guidance, navigation, timekeeping, pace notes and moral support, to mention but a few areas. The top teams and drivers have known it for a long time. Only recently have the public come to recognize the importance of the co-driver, through witnessing his contribution via the TV screen.

Co-driving techniques have been forced to advance along with the progress of cars, teams and drivers. One example of this is the map-reading technique employed here in the UK. Such was the perceived benefit of a UK-based co-driver read-

Left *Gavin Lodge.* (Lodge.)

Below *Les Kolczak.* (Kolczak.)

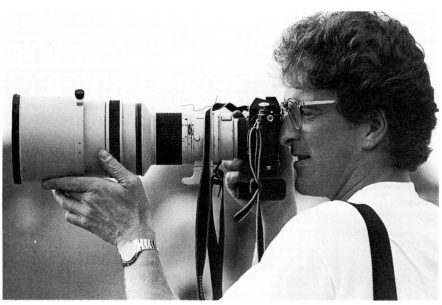

ing a stage off the map that first the Scottish and then the RAC Rally felt obliged to open their events up to reconnaissance and pace notes, so that outsiders would not feel disadvantaged through their unfamiliarity with our maps. The art of making good pace notes has also progressed, as well as the co-driver's input into the planning side of rallies—the service schedules and so on. Because of these advances, there are far more fully- or semi-professional co-drivers nowadays than, say, 10 or 20 years ago.

Because co-driving is becoming more identifiable in its own right, I believe more people are being attracted to the activity rather than falling into it by accident or by necessity. This book is aimed at all co-drivers—prospective, beginners, clubmen, national and international. It will take you from the very basics, through more serious rallying, right up to professional level. One thing I discovered in writing it is that there is so much to co-driving that it would be impossible, within the confines of these pages, to cover every single aspect, but hopefully I've touched on most of the important ones. I've also had to make various assumptions on occasions regarding resources (time and material) and the will to progress. I have used the masculine pronoun, not because of any chauvinism on my part, but because that comes from my own experience. I happen to believe that women make very good co-drivers, because of their light weight, clear voices and intuitive abilities, so I hope there is no offence taken, in these liberated days, if I don't perpetually write 'he/she' instead of just 'he'.

Let me also introduce my two principal photographers, Gavin Lodge and Les Kolczak. Neither is particularly well known, though their work is becoming increasingly displayed in a variety of motor sport magazines. Gavin is, like me, a Yorkshireman, whom I first met when I was just becoming a paid professional. He would frequently come to pick my brains about various matters on rallying and indeed is no mean co-driver himself, hence his grasp of the photographic subject matter which I required for the book. Les I met relatively recently, for he was the official team photographer during our successful years with Toyota GB. I well recall his ability to organize finish ramp ceremonies so that the best shots were taken, which was good for us, the team and its sponsors. Both Les and Gavin have that uncanny knack of being in the right place at the right time to get their photographs and I'm sure you'll see a lot more of their work in the coming years.

Aimed mainly at co-drivers this book may be, but I sincerely hope it will also be read by others within the sport. I trust drivers will read it, because many of them, I feel, don't really understand their co-driver or his function and consequently fail to get the best out of him. The same could be said for team managers and service crews and all the other people who come into contact with the person in the hot seat. As the book relates, there is a lot more to co-driving than meets the eye.

Co-driving has given me a lot of pleasure for some 25 years. It's also given me my fair share of excitement and incidents and amusing occurrences, which I wouldn't have missed for anything. If, through this book, I can kindle the same kind of enjoyment, excitement and dedication in others, then I shall be more than satisfied.

Part 1

CO-DRIVING BASICS

Chapter 1

In the beginning

Let me acquaint you with a little-known fact: co-drivers existed long before rallies were invented. At the turn of the century, when competition between drivers of the new-fangled motor cars began, there were almost invariably two people on board the car. The events were ostensibly 'trials', running from city to city (such as Paris–Bordeaux), which to the vehicles of the day were every bit a challenge on a par with some of our long-distance rallies of more recent times. These competitions soon 'degenerated' (if that is the correct term) into races, rather than the more stately progress which the organizers had in mind, but the presence of that extra person on board is interesting. What was his purpose? A back-up driver perhaps? A riding mechanic? Or was he a navigator, since even the 'main roads' between big cities could hardly have been well signposted or easy to find in those dim and distant days. Perhaps he was a combination of all three functions, but the similarities with the modern day co-driver are quite significant.

Public opinion soon forced these events off the public highway and on to tracks or closed roads, thus creating 'motor racing'. Interestingly, sports car racing has retained the principle of more than one driver even through to today, though these days they don't actually get into the car at the same time. One of the great sports car races of the 1950s, the Mille Miglia, did permit two persons on board and, as is well known, in 1955 the event was won by Stirling Moss in a Mercedes, with Denis Jenkinson reading what can only be described as pace notes. Moss confirmed the contribution the notes had made to his victory. They may not have been the first crew to prepare pace notes, but Moss's acknowledgement certainly proved their effectiveness, as well as the difference a good co-driver can make.

Even with the upsurge of interest in motor racing, there remained a demand for events using 'normal' cars, based on the public highway. These were still termed trials and were taken very seriously by manufacturers, and co-drivers (sometimes more than one) were required. The word 'rally' in the present context was not used until 1911, when the first Monte Carlo Rally took place, primarily as an attempt to boost trade in the Principality at a traditionally quiet time of year. Not only were co-drivers essential as relief drivers, on-board mechanics and navigators, but to judge from the photographs of the time, even the ladies of the crew were brought along, together with picnic hampers, champagne, flowers and all sorts of other paraphernalia.

Sporting drivers would soon tire of events where, apart from the challenge of getting there, the only competition was the Concours d'Élégance. So trials and rallies therefore began to include driving tests (we now call them Autotests) to sort out the winner. For many years, before and after the Second World War, rallies were resolved in this way. Co-drivers were generally kept on board for such activities, but apart from the navigation side, there is little evidence that they made any substantial contribution to the result. Where they did contribute was on the 'regularity' sections of rallies, ensuring that their drivers were neither too early, nor too late, over a given section.

Only in the 1950s, when endurance events over the more remote and rugged parts of Europe were taking place, did the co-driver start to make a really worthwhile impact. Events such as the Liege–Rome–Liege and the Alpine Rally came to be recognized by car manufacturers as good promotional tools for their products. The 'works' teams built better cars, with better equipment and back-up, spending more time on preparation and practice in the pursuit of success. Navigation, timekeeping and pace notes therefore acquired greater significance, if the expense was not to be wasted by some silly timekeeping or navigational error, or by the driver being caught out by some unexpected feature of the road.

While the virtual lack of traffic in remote areas allowed such speed-related events to continue for many years, other parts of Europe (led by Scandinavia and followed shortly by the RAC Rally in the UK) took to special stages, using closed roads, mostly in forests, and timed to the second. This development quickly gained ascendancy as the on-road 'thrashes' faced more and more adverse opinion from locals and the rapidly increasing motor population of Europe. The greater acceptability of closed road rallying, whether in forests or on public roads closed for the occasion, removed what remaining inhibitions manufacturers may have had about the sport, and the 'Golden Era' began. With the car makers' bigger involvement came greater opportunities for serious co-drivers, so that by the mid '60s fully professional co-drivers existed, i.e. those totally dependent on the sport for their living, rather than partly-paid amateurs. Recognition at last.

Of course, rallying is not all about works teams and professionals. It's also very much a sport for the privateer, in many parts of the world and particularly in the UK. For many years British rallying was based on the 'road rally', a competitive, timed event taking place mostly at night-time on open public roads. This version continued to flourish even after the introduction of forestry special stages, primarily because it was easy to get involved in (almost any car would do), it was cheap and it was tremendous fun. Alas, this wasn't to last and by the '80s was in serious decline as a result of legislation, in the face of mounting criticism by the authorities. By the '90s it was effectively dead, but in the meantime over its 30-year heyday this branch of rallying had spawned a whole crop of navigators who went on to succeed at all levels of special stage rallying.

Here we run into a bit of a dilemma, because what do you actually call the man (or woman) who sits alongside the rally driver? I would suggest that if he or she does purely navigational events, then it's 'navigator'; if the events contain special stages or involve high speed, then it's 'co-driver', but it's a very moot point. Certainly, with the demise of road rallying, the term 'co-driver' seems to have found greater favour. Yet even this is a misnomer, because unlike his forebears at the turn of the century, today's co-driver is unlikely to drive, nor does he need to (though at times he may) act as travelling mechanic. He will certainly need to be able to navigate, and timekeep, and do all the many jobs that the modern co-driver must do, but perhaps the problem is that within our language we do not have a single word for this occupation that accurately describes all its functions.

There are some similarities with other sports, but no exact parallel. A co-driver has been likened to the goal-keeper of a football team—the last line of defence after the rest of the team have given the ball away. There's a closer likeness to the golf caddy, the person who advises his player on the best line for a hole and the best club to play—though a driver who asks his co-driver to carry his bag of equipment around might get a rather blunt response. There's the passenger on a racing motorcycle combination—certainly the on-board presence is similar, but the contribution is more physical than mental, I suspect. Then there are the various coaches alongside the boxers, the tennis players, the athletes—but when it comes to the action, these people are left on the sideline. So perhaps it's a combination of all these elements, with a few other traits thrown in. Certainly no other sport that I can think of combines the preparation and mental input of the co-driver with the required in-car presence and subjection to risk—and excitement.

But then few people really understand what makes a co-driver 'tick' anyway. Certainly don't ask a driver—he's generally convinced that all co-drivers are stark, staring bonkers. I doubt if you would ever get a top driver to go co-driving. The odd occasion when they've been obliged to sit alongside another rally driver, perhaps for testing or on a press day, will usually cause them to vow never, ever to do that again. They just cannot comprehend how anyone can sit there and take all that lurching and swaying and jumping and going sideways and nearly crashing and so on *and* do the timekeeping and navigating, as well as calmly read out the pace notes, without going completely crazy. Drivers are often referred to as being 'brave', but perhaps it's the co-drivers who should be credited with the greater amount of 'bottle'.

So we can see that there's a difference in mental attitude between drivers and co-drivers. There are some exceptional characters who cross the divide either way, co-drivers who go driving and drivers who go co-driving. But generally the two 'breeds' stick to their own paths. I hesitate to categorize people, but generally the co-driver tends to be the quieter, more studious of the two, perhaps less extroverted than his driver, who as a rôle model is expected to be aggressive and flamboyant. But I can think of many exceptions, all successful, to both of these stereotypes.

Why do people become co-drivers in the first place? Mostly, it would appear, by accident. Few actually set out to be a co-driver, but circumstances seem to take them that way. I used to do a bit of driving (I even won a road event once) but the limited funds of a student meant that the only way I could stay in the rallying I had come to enjoy so much was to navigate for someone else. I soon found I could navigate quite well, other people got to know of it and I was on my way. Would I ever go back to rally driving? Well, I've co-driven for some pretty good drivers over the years, three of them World Rally Champions, and there's simply no way I could ever drive like they do. But co-drive for them? Yes, I could do that all day long. If you talk to other co-drivers, there are similar tales of how they got dragged into the job, but now wouldn't be separated from it.

It doesn't matter who or what you are, anybody can be a co-driver. Rally co-driving, I find, is totally classless: you can be male or female, white or coloured, rich or poor, big or small, able-bodied or disabled; it really makes little or no difference. On the question of size, a smaller co-driver is generally lighter than a bigger one, which is considered preferable (to a very small degree) for the power to weight ratio of the rally car. However, the important thing is that the co-driver should be effective. It's no good having the lightest co-driver around, if that co-driver makes a lot of errors. Arne Hertz, one of the most successful co-drivers ever, is certainly no lightweight, nor is double World Champion Juha Piironen, but that hasn't prevented their drivers from gaining a lot of success.

Of course, rally co-driving has its minus points. It's unsociable in terms of the weeks, hours and days of your (and your family's) time it takes up. It's often carried out in an uncomfortable, noisy, harsh environment. It frequently involves being out in unpleasant weather. It's hard work in terms of the preparation and sorting out you have to do. It can be dangerous (though in my view, not unacceptably so). There are cheaper sports. There are safer sports. There are sports which don't demand the same high level of commitment or gut-wrenching pressure. But for me, none of them have the attraction of rallying, particularly when you can enjoy the sport from the very heart of the action, inside the car.

What can possibly compare with hurtling along a snow-covered stage in Sweden at 100 mph, with the car just kissing the snow banks? Or flying for many metres over the jumps of the 1000 Lakes? Or charging through the bush on the Safari? Or hurtling down an Alpine pass, with the spectacular scenery of the Monte Carlo Rally rushing by? Or pounding over the rock-strewn tracks of Greece? Or seeing day break over the daunting wastes of Kielder Forest on a clear frosty November morning? The bark of the exhaust, the shrill whistles of the stage marshals, the clatter of stones under the wheel arches, the G-forces as the driver sets the car up sideways for a tight corner, the smell of mud caking on a hot exhaust. All these sights, sounds and experiences can be yours to enjoy when you go co-driving, and you don't have to be rich. You just have to be dedicated and with a bit of luck and perseverance, work your way up the co-driving ladder. It need not be a long haul.

Chapter 2

Early days

L et's assume you've decided you'd like to be a co-driver. How are you going to go about 'getting a ride', as we sometimes call it? Your first move should be to join a suitable motor club. There are lots of motor clubs in the UK and these are governed by the Royal Automobile Club Motor Sports Association (RACMSA). Just about anyone can set up a motor club, so it's quite possible that there are some clubs which are not affiliated to the RACMSA and which are therefore referred to as 'pirate' clubs. My advice would be to give these a very wide berth indeed; not only may their events be illegal in certain respects, but your participation in them could be prejudicial to your future motor sport activities. In any case there are so many legitimate clubs to choose from, catering for a wide range of interests, that it should be possible for you, wherever you live, to find what you're looking for.

The 'Blue Book'

The RAC MSA publishes a book, known in the sport as the 'Blue Book' (officially the *RAC MSA Motor Sports Year Book*), which is full of all sorts of information about the organization of motor sports. We're going to refer to it several times in this and later chapters, so as it tends to be a regular part of a co-driver's equipment it's probably a good idea to get hold of one straight away. If you know someone already active in motor sport, you can perhaps borrow their copy, but sooner or later you'll have to get your own. When you apply for a competition licence, for events beyond the confines of your local club, you get one anyway, along with regular bulletins about events and rule changes. So it's well worth having one, but you don't actually have to buy it just yet. At this stage, you really only need it to check on the motor clubs in your area.

Unfortunately, while the Blue Book conveniently lists clubs by regions, it doesn't actually tell you the particular motor sport activity in which each club specializes. In some cases this is obvious: for instance, some clubs cater for just one make of car, but generally these clubs don't organize the type of rally we're interested in here: the British Automobile Racing Club (BARC) would not be likely to organize rallies (though in fact they used to in the past), but the British Trials and Rally Drivers' Association (BTRDA, an influential rally-orientated club) might offer better possibilities. However both these clubs are fairly large national organizations (of which there are several) and so not really the sort of club a beginner should be looking at to begin co-driving. More likely, you'll be seeking a local club, which might be titled the 'So & So and District Motor Club'. If you happen to live in or near 'So & So', then it could benefit you to call up the secretary of the club (as listed in the Blue Book) and ask him/her about the club and its activities. To be honest, many motor clubs nowadays are organized primarily for social gatherings, for people with a common but peripheral interest in motor cars and not necessarily in the sporting side. There is nothing wrong with that; with the high cost of participation these days, you can hardly blame people for not getting involved in serious competition. The secretary's description may well indicate this kind of club, and if you like the idea of such convivial gatherings, then do join. However, while you may have a jolly time and meet a lot of nice people,

The Blue Book—the RAC MSA's Motor Sports Yearbook.

perhaps you will find it hard to become a co-driver within such a club, if they don't actually run or get involved with any rallies.

A rallying club

It may be that your local club does run some small navigation events, however, so as well as enjoying the social side of things, you can have a go at these 'rallies', which can be a lot of fun as well as give you a low pressure introduction to the rudiments of navigating and timekeeping. Another important point is that your chosen motor club should be one which is invited by other clubs to compete in their rallies, otherwise you end up having to join another club just to get an entry. Once you do National level events or above, the club membership rule doesn't apply (though on some Nationals and even Internationals you are occasionally required to state to which club you belong), but until then you do need this facility, so please check. It is important to get on the right track at this point. To enable you to make your choice, it would certainly help to ask someone you know who does a bit of rallying which is the best club for that branch of the sport in your particular area. Alternatively, if you know of a rally taking place nearby, go along and ask the organizers or competitors about a good local club. They may be rather preoccupied with the event at the time, but will probably point you in the right direction. Sometimes it's worth travelling a bit further afield to belong to an active rallying club, rather than sticking to a low-profile local one. Unlike golf clubs, motor clubs are not expensive to join; you certainly won't be put on a waiting list. There's nothing to stop you joining more than one, if that will give you the rallying and social activities you seek.

Club events

So, armed with your new club membership card, you can now begin to participate. The club newsletter will usually tell you what events are about to take place and will either include the necessary entry forms or tell you where you can get them. Go along to the next club night and get to know some of the other members; almost invariably they'll be a friendly bunch and will be well disposed towards newcomers. They'll certainly let you know what's coming up, if only to 'persuade' you to come along and marshal. A good motor club will have plenty of things going on every month and as a newcomer I suggest you do as many events as you can at this stage. It doesn't matter if it's an autotest, production car trial, treasure hunt, economy run

Above *A Motor Club Membership Card—essential for basic competitions.*

Right *A typical club newsletter—full of information about forthcoming events.*

or navigational rally. I certainly wouldn't rule out doing some events as a driver, but even if you don't have a car, you can get involved in most things, either as a passenger/navigator or as a marshal/observer or helping the organizers. The main thing is that you get experience of how motor competitions are run, and enjoy yourself. If the club mans a stage on a rally, this too is a good way of learning about the sport, as well as seeing some action at close quarters. The fact that the weather is awful or you get bitten by countless midges or you end up covered in mud is immaterial. At least when you move into serious competition yourself, you'll appreciate even more the efforts of the marshals, without whom no rally could take place.

Marshalling on rallies is a good way of learning about the sport.

Navigational events

We all have to start somewhere and for most people that starting point is a club navigational rally. At the club night, if you let it be known that you're wanting to do some navigating, almost invariably someone sooner or later will want to take you along. Usually, it's a question of a driver trying to coerce someone to sit alongside him, so a willing partner is almost sure to find a ride without too much trouble. Navigators are not very plentiful, especially good, keen ones, but at this stage you can hardly expect to get a call from the club champion. More likely, your first driver will be a novice like yourself, so in this case you'll both be going through the learning process together. That's not a bad thing, because it takes a bit of pressure off you and perhaps you won't be alone in making a fool of yourself.

Club events have been subject to ever more restrictions in recent years. 'Road rallying' as it was known, which for a long time was the backbone of speed-related club rally sport, has been effectively legislated out of existence as a result of pressures from local inhabitants, farmers and the police. I don't propose to go into the arguments for and against this—the issue is history now anyway—but the point is, don't expect your club rally to be a classic event of speed and endurance. Most 'rallies' at this level will be just for fun, be it a treasure hunt, a navigational scatter or an economy run. Such are the variations of these events that this book could no doubt be filled with their details, but that is hardly the aim; nor is it my intention to spoil the fun and novelty of these situations by 'spilling the beans' on the organizers' intricacies. Like everyone else, you'll just have to muddle your way through, getting caught out, lost and thoroughly confused. Again, it's all part of the learning process, and usually good fun. My only guidance for this aspect of co-driving is that you take along with you a map-board (for safety reasons make this flexible), the local map(s), several pencils, a rubber, a reliable watch, perhaps a map magnifier and as devious a mind as you can muster. It's all good experience, but in time you will probably want to move on to something more realistic.

Depending on your area, you may be fortunate to find some pure navigational rallies, where you will certainly be able to sharpen your skills upon map and watch. While these are no longer the challenges they once were, they are certainly well worth doing. You will however need a 'Restricted' Competition Licence if the event is above 'Closed' status (see Chapter 3).

Not only will you learn to plot a route with speed and accuracy, but you will also need to run to a specific average speed and achieve time controls at specific times—not late, not early and not waiting outside the control for the time to come up. This is known as 'regularity'. If you can do some of these, they're well worth the effort to give you navigational and time-keeping practice. Some people develop a fascination for this type of thing, but without wishing to detract from the fun and challenge of such rallies, I suspect the budding co-driver (as opposed to pure navigator) will want rather more than this.

Map references

With events on the public highway being controlled to run at an average speed of 30 mph or less and with even the humblest motor car being capable of maintaining such a speed over almost any surfaced road, the scope for running some sort of competitive event on the public highway is severely limited. So some clubs run 'table top rallies' which take place indoors and which enable you to plot a route on a map, against the clock, given certain information. These too may entail a bit of the treasure hunt mentality, but they do give you a basic understanding of maps as well as practice in using them, which are very important aspects of a co-driver's craft.

If you didn't do map references in Geography at school, or weren't paying attention when you should have been, then now is the time to redress the situation. In this country we're

Essential for rapid plotting, Romers come in various sizes and specifications.

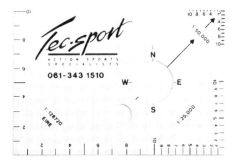

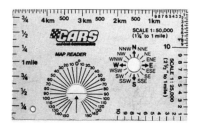

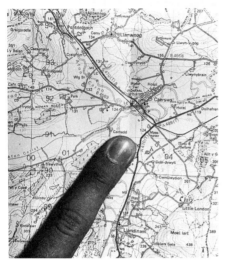

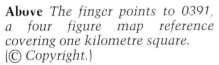

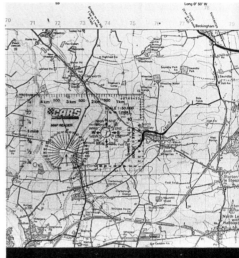

Above *The finger points to 0391, a four figure map reference covering one kilometre square.* (© *Copyright.*)

Above right *Plotting a map reference.* (Lodge.) (© *Copyright.*)

Right *You may not need a map magnifier or 'poti' just yet.* (Kolczak.)

blessed with an excellent map system provided by the Ordnance Survey. Only when one does rallies in some other countries does one realize just how good our British maps are. The detail here is excellent and the information provided is extensive. Primarily the 1:50,000 series is the base map for rallies, but in time you will have some use for the 1:250,000 and 1:25,000 series. Each map tells you how to plot a map reference and to help you do this quickly and accurately, I suggest you get yourself a 'Romer', which you can find at most map shops. This small piece of plastic takes the guesswork out of map reference plotting. For British rallies you will find yourself using it regularly.

Basically, it works this way: the whole of the country is divided into a grid and each map contains a section of that grid. On a 1:50,000 map that grid is generally defined by 40 numbers along the top and bottom edges of the map and by 40 numbers along the left and right edges of the map. I mention them specifically in that order, because that is the order in which you use the numbers. 'Along the passage' (the numbers along the bottom edge) 'and up the stairs' (the numbers along the side edge) is the mnemonic to get you to remember to plot in this way; there was one rally I did (it had to be in Ireland) where the organizers had mistakenly plotted every reference 'up the stairs and along the passage' so that the majority of their time controls, if plotted conventionally, were located in the middle of fields, mountains and the Irish Sea. The bulletin correcting this misapprehension was, I recall, wonderful in its explanation.

A four-figure number is a map reference in itself: 0391 is the kilometre square to which the finger points in the photograph. Sometimes this reference is used to define a 'no-go zone' or a 'quiet zone', but generally a kilometre square on its own is far too coarse a definition for rallying, where we need to know the exact position of something. So the Romer effectively divides each kilometre square into 100 little blocks by splitting each horizontal line into tenths of a kilometre (100 metres) and likewise each vertical line. It's important that you use the corner of the Romer relevant to the scale of map you are using (1:50,000 in this example).

Let's say we have the map reference 120/755875. Dispensing with the map number (120), we first split the reference in half, 755 and 875. Take the first two figures of each half—in this case 75 and 87—to find the kilometre square and then place the Romer's top edge number 5 along the vertical line 75. Run it up or down that line until you come to the horizontal 87 line and place the Romer's side edge number 5 on this line. Assuming the top edge is still correctly aligned, the top right corner of the Romer is now pointing at our required map reference. Bingo. This sounds complicated but with a little practice it becomes second nature. Mind you, this reference can still be a little coarse in some situations (it does after all cover a 100-metre square), so you might get a figure 754½ 875¼: the fractions break down our 100-metre square into half and then a quarter respectively. The same process works on the other scale Ordnance Survey maps, but of course their squares are a different size because of their different scale. Nevertheless, the reference will plot in the same place, whatever the map scale.

If you need to find the map reference of a particular point, you simply reverse the process: place the point of the Romer on the required location and read off the two vertical grid numbers plus the Romer's top line number, followed by the two horizontal grid numbers plus the Romer's side line number, adding ½ or ¼ if required. Don't forget to add the map number on the front of the reference, if necessary. If you feel unaccustomed to plotting map references, a little practice will do no harm. You can send off for correspondence courses on navigation, covering this and other topics; they are advertised in the motor sporting press. Some people like to use a map magnifier—for blind forest rallying I would say it's essential—but at this stage you don't need to spend a lot of money. If you have any eyesight difficulties however, you might find one useful; the motor sporting press carry adverts for them and in any case we'll take a closer look at them later. By handling maps regularly and taking part in events you will soon be able to plot your way around without difficulty.

Map marking

Maps are something to value so you should look after them. When marking, use a soft pencil—a B or 2B—which makes a bold mark but is easily cleaned off. If you use a harder pencil than this—an H or 2H—it not only tends to dig into the map and tear the paper, it is also difficult to rub out later, so the map is spoiled. For the same reason, never, ever use a pen on a map; most co-drivers regard this as sacrilege. The only problem with a 2B is that its softness makes the point blunt rather quickly, so you need a good supply of them, or to be a deft hand with the sharpener. Already we seem to be accumulating a certain amount of navigating kit—pencils, rubber, sharpener, Romer—so it makes sense to keep it safe and tidy in a small pencil case or similar, in which you will accumulate other useful small oddments. One final point: never travel with a pen or pencil in your mouth; the prospect of swallowing it when the car goes over a bump is too realistic to be amusing.

Watch

The next piece of equipment you'll need is a good accurate watch. Let me show my age by saying that when I started rallying, digital watches just weren't available. I used a chronograph with a stop-watch facility and I must admit it served me very well. Some people still prefer to use this type of watch face. There are occasionally some problems with reading such a watch accurately, so you have to stay alert, particularly when the second hand is close to the full minute mark.

This difficulty was quite often the cause of one-minute errors made by the timekeepers on events, which led to frequent post-event discussions. However, the advent of the digital watch changed all that. The large digital clocks with freeze display used by timekeepers eliminated most (but not all) of the human errors associated with official timing, while the facilities offered by the average wristwatch multiplied as far as the co-driver was concerned. The choice nowadays is quite stagggering, with all sorts of features available to give you timing and other information. Personally I would advise against buying one with too many features; for instance, a built-in calculator might appear to be useful, but the watch becomes too cluttered and therefore fiddly to use at times of pressure. The use of the watch needs to be second nature to you; you shouldn't need a degree in electronics to work out how to use it—its use should be instinctive to you. If you have to think about how to stop or start the stop-watch facility, you'll probably get it wrong at a critical point. So, try to find a watch which is fairly straightforward, is easy to read and operate, has a stop-watch facility and a clear LCD face, some illumination and is reasonably durable with a strong strap. I did once substitute my regular digital watch for a different, less substantial type but which had more features; when we had to stop mid-stage and change a puncture in a hurry, the strap broke and the watch flew off. It's probably still working away in the ditch now, but that wasn't a lot of use to me at the time.

Below left *A typical digital wrist watch incorporating a stop-watch facility.* (Lodge.)

Below right *A digital watch on a cord—bigger figures but it can swing around during a special stage and cause distraction.* (Lodge.)

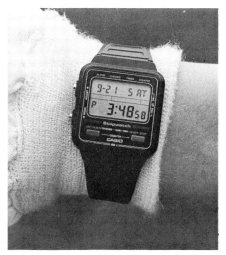

Some people like to have one of those larger stop-watches on a cord hanging round their necks. It may look like a good piece of kit—certainly the big numbers are handy for easy reading—but in a car it can swing and sway around causing distraction and even injury, so I would advise you to go for the wrist type.

Timing

Having now got your watch, perhaps you should understand something of timing systems. With the demise of road rallying, some of the trickier types of timekeeping have gone. We are now principally concerned with the actual time of day, to which all timepieces—organizers' and competitors'—should be set. Before you start and whatever the event, it's always as well to check that your watch time coincides with that of the organizers. The general principle is that a minute continues for 60 seconds. That may sound obvious, but in rallying terms the minute of, say, 14:36 continues from 14:36 and 00 seconds through to 14:36 and 59.9 seconds. Once the second has gone on to 14:37 and 00 seconds, you're into the next minute. It's important to recognize this tolerance that you have, as well as to realize that at 14:35 and 59 seconds you are early and at 14:37 and 00 seconds you are late.

Few rallies these days are determined specifically by the road timing, but results can be affected by road penalties, so you need to become accustomed to looking after the timekeeping and understand its workings. Some grasp of the general passage of time is useful; this will develop as you gain experience, but if you are the sort of person who is perennially late for appointments you will perhaps have to make a bigger effort in this direction. Remember, on rallies the clock is running all the time and few, if any, excuses for lateness are tolerated. Once you progress to special stages, the timing is done to the second (hence the need for a stop watch), but we'll come to that in a later chapter.

Paperwork

Paperwork is another area of co-driving that you'll have to master. At this stage of the game, it's not too difficult to understand. You'll need to be able to fill in event entry forms accurately and completely. To do this you need to have read and understood the event regulations. It still surprises me how many would-be co-drivers fail to do this. It doesn't surprise me that things go wrong as a result. If you're not sure of the meaning of something, check with the organizers. On the

It's always a good idea to check that the time on your watch coincides with that of the organizers, before the start. (Lodge)

event don't forget to take your club membership card with you and any other paperwork the event might demand. It's a question of getting used to handling such things as a matter of course; as a co-driver, people will expect you to do this.

Moving on

So far, we've just touched on the basics of fun rallies within the motor club. Hopefully, you will want to go further. Some people miss this phase out altogether, with little detriment to their co-driving career. At this stage you should be like a sponge, soaking up everything relevant you come into contact with. Read the motor sporting press; *Motoring News* and *Autosport* come out weekly and are full of news and information. There are other monthly magazines with varying amounts of rally coverage. Reports on events are interesting—you can learn how people got it wrong and how they got it right. That knowledge may be of use to you in the future. News of forthcoming events is useful—there may be a bigger event soon in your area which you might like to go and see. The advertisements are worth reading, not just for cars but also parts, equipment, events and opportunities. Right now, you should be looking to lay your hands on every piece of rally information you can get. Read rally books, borrow the road books of past rallies, talk to experienced competitors, go to rally forums, go to local rallies. The list is endless. Now is the time to absorb as much basic information as possible so that you can move on to the next step. Hopefully by now you've been well and truly bitten by the rallying bug and are keen to get involved in something a little more challenging and a little more exciting.

Chapter 3

Getting organized

G etting organized is the basis of a lot of your co-driving. So while you may well be anxious to get on with the rallying, it will pay you to do a bit of planning and some background work before going out on a proper event. We have to make a few assumptions: that you've found yourself a driver through your local motor club, that you've acquired a basic understanding of maps, timekeeping and so on (we'll spend some more time on these aspects later), and that you have some funds available to pay your expenses. Let us also assume that you are now looking primarily at special stage events as the way to go forward and develop your co-driving.

Licences

While your trusty club membership card is sufficient for events open only to members of that club, and for you as a non-driving navigator for 'Clubman' events, it's now about time for you to go ahead and get your Competition Licence. You might not need it if your first event is a 'Closed to Club' rally, but a 'Restricted' may be in your plans, so ask the RAC MSA to send you an application form. Inevitably, because the document concerns matters of responsibility and importance, there are some fairly weighty questions to be answered. However, they're straightforward enough, so make sure you answer them truthfully, correctly and in full. Of course, the RAC MSA will wish you to part with money for your Restricted Competition Licence (even more if you are in a hurry), but in return you will receive a computer-printed document in a plastic cover, together with your 'Blue Book' which we mentioned in Chapter 2. You'll also receive at regular intervals the bulletin, which keeps you up to date with rule changes, tribunals, and other events.

Incidentally, if you don't drive or don't anticipate driving as a co-driver, you can apply for a Navigator/Non-Driver Licence, so long as you accept its limitations. Like the standard licence, this can be upgraded to give you access to bigger status events in the future. If you need the option to drive, then apply for the Rally (Driver) Licence—you can use it as a co-driver. The rules for upgrading in the early 1990s are that you need to finish four Clubman or Restricted rallies to upgrade from Restricted to National and one National rally or two further Restricteds (of the special stage variety) to upgrade from National to International. Proof of finishing is a signature on the reverse of the licence by the Clerk of the Course. No finish—no signature. Don't be in too much of a hurry to upgrade. It's going to cost you extra money for the higher grades but while it may be a good 'pose' in the club to have a new International licence, there are no bonuses for getting it in record time, so only upgrade when the time is right. However, as you gain experience, you don't want to have to turn down a good National or even International 'ride' just because you don't have the correct grade, so keep the situation under review.

Most beginners in the rallying game are private entrants, that is, their car is entered by themselves, or more correctly, in the name of the driver. You can carry a limited amount of

You will soon need an RAC MSA Competition Licence. This is an International Licence, and includes the visa necessary for competing in foreign International rallies (see Chapter 12).

*Only limited advertising is permitted without an Advertising Permit.
(Kolczak.)*

advertising (basically five small decals each side plus a windscreen strip) on the basis of the driver's Competition Licence, but you cannot otherwise plaster the car with advertising. If your car has a sponsor and you wish to enter the car in the name of a firm, organization or person who will not drive, then you will need an Entrants Licence. This will cost you some more money that you must pay to the RAC MSA, and even with this licence the amount of advertising you can carry is similarly limited. For details, see the Blue Book.

Though it is unlikely at this point, if you wish to carry advertising on the rally car beyond these limits then you also need an Advertising Permit, the cost of which varies depending on the grade of events you are doing. Such matters are more in the driver's province, but he may not be aware of the somewhat involved rules on this, so you need to know the score, if

*With this amount of advertising, Phil Collins' Ford Sierra Cosworth
would certainly require an Advertising Permit. (Lodge.)*

only to save a lot of embarrassment at scrutineering. Clearly, if you don't have the correct licence for the advertising, you will have to remove it or cover it up, which looks messy and will hardly impress your new sponsor. The arrival of a sponsorship cheque of £100 from your local 'chippy' is not a lot of help if you find you have to pay £120 to the RAC MSA for the right to emblazon the chippy's name large on the car. However, at this stage you are probably better off staying as a private entrant, because many events carry awards aimed specifically at this group of competitors. The one exception to the Entrants Licence rule is when you are entered by your own motor club. Clubs quite often put in their own team of cars, either for publicity, which comes with success, or because there's a local inter-club championship for which they need points. In this case you can use the club's Entrants Licence (the club gets them free), but you are still bound by the normal advertising rules.

The rules

Now you've got your own 'Blue Book', take time to study it carefully. No, not every word from cover to cover, because it's not exactly the world's most enthralling text. Many of its sections cover other unrelated branches of motor sport, or organizers' procedures, which don't immediately concern you. Seek out the sections which do matter and read them through. Competition Organization, Competition Regulations and Technical Regulations are all areas you need to know about, especially the sub-sections which concern rallies. Be ready to take advice. If you don't know the meaning of something, ask an experienced competitor or organizer in your club. That way you'll be more confident on events through a better understanding of the rules. It's easy to be caught out by the rules, especially if you don't understand them in the first place.

The regulations

The sort of event you're most likely to tackle first is probably a single- or multi-venue special stage event. Depending on your area, you may be blessed with an abundance of this type of rally (disused airfields and quarries are likely locations), or they may be few and far between. Unlike forestry events, the cost of using the venue is low, so the entry fee is also lower. The demand for entries is correspondingly higher. This is partly due to costs and partly to vehicle regulations. The higher up the rallying scale you climb, the more restrictive are the rules

Above left *The slightly artificial, but nevertheless enjoyable, terrain of a typical single- or multi-venue special stage event.* (Lodge.)

Above right *Regulations for foreign International, British Open and British Club rallies.*

about the sort of car you can use. But for your single/multi-venue event, virtually anything goes, as long as the car complies with the safety requirements. So most rally cars are eligible, even older ones, and therefore entries will generally be full.

You need to get your hands on a set of regulations at an early stage. Ask for two sets—one for you, one for the driver. Having studied them carefully, fill in the entry form fully and accurately, though you will need some input from your driver to do this. Note that I'm suggesting that you manage this aspect, because drivers are notoriously unreliable creatures when it comes to form filling and other paperwork. You will need details of the car from the driver—registration number, engine size, specification (production or modified), insurance arrangements, past results—as well as some form of payment. I'll come back to the costs aspect later. Having double-checked that all is complete, keep a photocopy of the form and send the entry off (better still, deliver it personally) to the entries secretary in good time. Most importantly, state on the entry form (even if the organizers don't provide space for it) that you wish all correspondence to come to you. Quite a few events provide self-adhesive labels for this purpose. It's no earthly good the final instructions being sent to your entrant/sponsor (the local chippy?) and not much better their being sent to your driver, who may well lose them or forget to pass them on to you until just before the start. Then is not the time

Entry forms are generally straightforward, but make sure you fill them in completely and accurately.

to discover that you need an extra map not specified in the regulations.... So, make sure all the stuff comes to you; you can always make a photocopy of any relevant paperwork to pass on to the driver, as there may be some technical points therein that he needs to attend to.

I'm sorry to go on about getting the entry form filled in correctly, but if you speak to any organizers, they will tell you the same old story: forms that are barely legible, forms with important information missing, wrong class of car quoted, no past results (so 'seeding' the entry will be difficult), no cheque, incorrectly dated cheque, dud cheque, forms submitted late— the list is endless. If you can turn in a full, clear, accurate entry form, first of all you're going to endear yourself to the organizers (which may be to your advantage later), secondly, you're more likely to get an entry in the case of over-subscription, and thirdly, you might get a better seeding than others who have been lax in this respect. It's well worth the effort.

Costs

This is an area which can cause problems between driver and co-driver, so it's a good idea to get financial matters straightened out at an early stage. That way there should be no misunderstandings and recriminations later. You don't need me to tell you that rallying is a very expensive sport. As a co-driver, your financial input will not be as great as that of the driver, but you should expect to take on some of the costs. There are no hard and fast rules on this, unfortunately, so you'll have to negotiate. There is a tendency for drivers to suggest that co-drivers suffer from short arms and long pockets—in some cases not without cause—but drivers too can be a little bit mean and expect a co-driver to bear an unreasonable proportion of the costs. Obviously, the driver has the capital costs of the rally car to sustain, as well as the equipping and maintenance of it. Also, if he crashes it, he suffers financially as a result. On the other hand, as you will discover if you gain success, it's the driver who gets the glory, so he should expect to pay more than you.

The point is, a driver should normally plan to carry these costs anyway (as he would have to in, say, racing, where no co-driver is involved), so any cost-sharing should normally be restricted to the 'on event' costs. These include entry fee, insurance, petrol (to, from and on event) food, service crew costs, tyres and other consumables and accommodation (if the event is too far away to reach in one day). Sit down together and do a mini-budget for the rally. I cannot say that you should split these costs 50/50 or 70/30 or in any particular way; it really depends on your own and your driver's circumstances. With one of my drivers, I had an arrangement that I would pay only for the petrol and he would cover the rest; so if we finished the rally, my costs were higher than if we retired. With another, just the entry fee and insurance, plus my own costs of maps, equipment, travel, etc. In that case my costs were the same, win, lose or draw. With others, we just split the on-event costs down the middle.

Through your own work or business, you may have some way of helping with a particular need for the rally effort. You might have access to a vehicle which can be used as a service van; your wife/girlfriend might be an excellent cook and can provide food and refreshment for the day. You might have a contact in the tyre trade who can do a good deal on the rubber. All these things are contributions of value and should be taken into account, but only on a pre-agreed basis, so there are no petty arguments later about who contributed this and who was expected to pay for that. The main aim is to come to an arrangement with which you're both reasonably satisfied.

Prizes

There was a time when prize money entered into such driver/co-driver discussions, but as organizers struggle to balance their own books, prize funds have shrunk considerably, almost to non-existence. So I'm sorry to disappoint those of you who thought that rallying was a way to riches. If there is any money to be won it will usually be quite a small amount and offered to a particular class or category (e.g. private entrants, production cars). Still, it's as well to discuss it, if only to agree that any prize money will go towards the service crew's bar bill (which will inevitably be a large one, in my experience). As far as trophies are concerned, you can expect to collect an award if there is one made to the co-driver, otherwise it will be just one for the driver. He might let you borrow it for a month or so, if he's considerate.

Trade bonuses, though not generally applicable to this grade of event, are a different matter. As they generally relate to the make of car or the equipment used thereon, these should rightly belong to the driver, as he's paying the preparation costs. In all probability he'll need the bonuses to fund the preparation for the next rally. Of course, you might strike it very lucky and go rallying with a super-rich or fully sponsored driver, who pays all your expenses with no quibble at all. Realistically, however, you can't expect to arrive at this situation until you are (a) very good and (b) a good deal further up the rallying ladder. But one can dream.

Insurance

This too is an area which requires a little bit of forethought. There are several aspects to consider. There's the event organizers' legal liability—this doesn't really concern us directly, but remember what I said about 'pirate' clubs in Chapter 2. Then there's the third party liability—towards landowners, other motorists and members of the public, etc. Also there's damage to the car and its occupants.

The organizers' responsibility is covered by the RAC MSA and that is clearly stated in the event's regulations. Basically this means that if you are involved in an accident while competing on private property, the RAC MSA's master policy covers you against claims from other parties.

If you take the trouble to read a standard motor insurance policy, I'm sure you will come across an exclusion for 'racing, pacemaking, reliability trials, speed testing or rallies'. Even if the wording is not quite so specific, your driver should check with his insurance company, because usually they will take exception to his submitting the vehicle they insure to what they will see as an added risk. Failure to advise them could well be treated as 'failing to disclose a material fact', thereby invalidating the insurance. However tempting it may be to skate around the edges of rally insurance, my advice would be—don't. It would be all too easy for an accident to happen and for your driver to face substantial damages for uninsured losses. Perhaps someone else's life could be ruined as a result. Insurance is important.

If your driver's insurance company or broker won't accommodate third party insurance for you while on the rally, then you can always apply for the Bowring Rally Scheme, which the RAC MSA's brokers arrange. For payment of a fee, you get cover for the event. Once again, details are in the Blue Book and the event's regulations will make some reference to it. So make sure this important aspect is attended to well before the rally.

Note that I stated 'third party insurance'. If your driver has comprehensive car insurance, he might be able to extend that to road section rally use, albeit on payment of further monies and/or with an increased accidental damage excess. If not, then you're stuck with paying your own damage in the event of an accident on the public highway. Clearly there is a much greater risk of damage while competing on special stages off the public highway and I doubt that your driver, however silver-tongued, will be able to persuade his insurance company

Full rally car insurance is expensive, but sometimes worthwhile. (Kolczak.)

to cover comprehensively for that (though I do know of some who have succeeded in this quest). The vast majority of competitors accept that situation as part of the sport and when the crunch comes, pay up for the repairs and probably retire gracefully for a while.

However, it *is* possible to get insurance on some of the value of the car for competition on special stages. This is very expensive and won't cover the total cost of repairs; there'll be a substantial accidental damage excess as well as a top limit beyond which the insurers won't pay, so you can't claim for a small 'ding' and you're not covered for a total write-off if, say, the car burned out. But some people pay it because of the value of their car or because they have a commitment to a championship and/or sponsor and need to know they can honour that commitment even if they have a big shunt. The Blue Book gives you the names of companies who take on this kind of risk.

Finally, you should give some thought to your personal insurance. The fact of competing on rallies may cause you to fall foul of certain exclusion clauses in whatever life insurance policies you hold. Companies vary so much; in my experience, some object to the very thought of you undertaking any sort of motor sport (few of them know what a rally is), while others seem totally unconcerned. If you have a mortgage linked to a life assurance policy, there could be some restriction on motor sport, so please check, and advise/amend where necessary; some modest increase in premium may be required in certain cases. That way your nearest and dearest are still covered

For special stages the rally car must have an approved roll-cage. Note the padding on the exposed sections. (Lodge.)

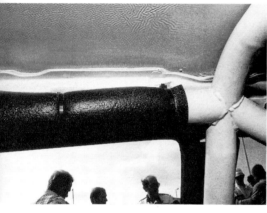

Padding is essential on the upper part of the roll-cage if you are not to hit your head or helmet on it. (Kolczak.)

should the unthinkable occur. Personal accident cover against death, injury and disability is available should you require it; again, contact the companies shown in the Blue Book.

After that, perhaps we should pass on to less sombre matters.

The car

I'm not going to go into a detailed description of rally car preparation, because that falls outside the scope of a book on co-driving and in any case is well covered elsewhere. Nor am I about to suggest a fully equipped works style co-driver's cockpit, because clearly that would be unnecessary for our small event. What we do need to do is establish a few basic essentials, so that we can sit there in relative safety and do the job of co-driving properly.

To some extent it depends on the base from which you are starting, i.e. has the car been rallied before or are you starting from scratch? Once again, turn to the Blue Book, which tells

Right *A competition seat is desirable but not essential at this stage. Note the six-point harness, with the crutch straps passing through the lower hole.* (Lodge.)

Below *Where's the circuit-breaker? Make sure you can reach it in an emergency.* (Lodge.)

you what you must have and also recommends what you should have, but which isn't compulsory.

Let's look at safety matters first. A roll cage is an essential item, for obvious reasons; this must be in accordance with the RAC MSA specifications. They're pretty unyielding items so at places where they run close to parts of your anatomy, I would suggest you have some padding attached to the pipework. The tube above the door is where you will sometimes clatter your head (with and without helmet), while the bar along the door space (if fitted) is just the place to bash your elbow or leg. You can get lengths of suitable tube padding—it looks a bit like the insulation used by plumbers for water pipes, but should be made of a fireproof material.

The seat is of prime importance to the co-driver. If it's a standard production seat, it should have a headrest to RAC MSA specification and it must be made not to slide, tilt, hinge or fold. So it's a question of getting the seat into the right position for you and then disabling the various adjustment mechanisms (it's surprising what you can do with a few jubilee clips). It's much better if the seat is a competition seat, for it will do none of those undesirable things and will have an integral head restraint, so it's merely a question of getting the location right for you and, very importantly, the seat itself securely mounted to the floor of the car. The scrutineer will check this with a fairly hefty tug, so it's as well to get it sorted properly now. If the seat wobbles, or pulls out of a rusty car floor, you can be sure you won't be getting past scrutineering—and rightly so.

Seat belts can be three-, four-, five- or six-point fixing—in my experience the more straps the better. The object is to locate you as securely as possible in the seat. Not only will you be safer for being properly belted in, but also you will feel more comfortable and relaxed and will therefore do your job better. Broader belts will spread the loads better and perhaps be more comfortable, but you can also get purpose-made shoulder pads to fit over the belts which will prevent them chafing or cutting into you in the event of a sharp impact.

Other essential safety items are:

Electrical circuit breaker—make sure you know where it is and how it works.

Fire extinguisher(s)—where they are, how they work, and check they're full. (By the way, on the event you must ensure that the safety pins are out, so that the trigger can be activated.)

Left *Make sure you know how to operate the fire extinguisher(s). This is the hand-held type. I'm not sure that it's wise to put the headsets just there though...* (Kolczak.)

Top right *This is the plumbed-in type of fire extinguishing system. Make sure the safety pin is out once the competition is under way.* (Kolczak.)

Air horns—capable of being operated by the co-driver (by a button on your side of the car).

Warning triangle, First Aid kit, SOS/OK board—all securely stowed but accessible.

Helmet, overalls, etc.

That takes care of the compulsory in-car items, but what else do you need? Clearly, a crash helmet, again complying with

Right *Many drivers prefer the better ventilation of an open-face helmet. Tommi Makinen, 1000 Lakes Rally, 1991. (Kolczak.)*

Right *The better sound insulation of a full-face helmet is preferred by many co-drivers. Lars Backman, 1000 Lakes Rally, 1991. (Kolczak.)*

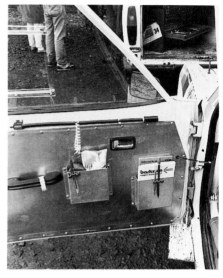

Above *Helmets can be stored on hooks...* (Lodge.)

Below *...or in nets...* (Lodge.)

Below *...or in fireproof foam boxes.* (Lodge.)

RAC MSA specifications. Some people prefer the lighter weight and better ventilation of an open-face type, others like the greater protection of a full-face type. Personally, I favour the full-face helmet, because when it comes to using an intercom I think it cuts out some of the extraneous noise, of which there will be plenty. But it's all a matter of personal preference and the only way you're going to get it right is to go to a specialist motor sport shop where they sell many different types and try them all. Fit is very important too. There should be no side to side movement, nor should you be able to pull the fastened helmet off by pulling forwards over your head from the rear. It should be close fitting but comfortable. Don't buy a helmet for the look, buy it for its suitability for you. Once you've got it, take it to a local RAC MSA scrutineer for checking. If he's happy with it, he'll put a special sticker on it. If he's not, at least you've time to take it back to where you bought it to change it for an approved type. It is better to discover this now than at scrutineering.

At this stage I wouldn't bother with an intercom, but we'll look at them later in the book. If your driver has a noisy car and a desire to hear your dulcet tones, he may however wish to invest in an intercom at this early stage.

One thing I would consider is stowage for the helmets. If you've just spent good money on a new helmet, the last thing you want is to have it rolling around the back of the car on a road section, getting knocked about and scratched. You can hang the helmets on hooks (I feel these can damage the earpieces/microphone should you have an intercom), or in nets, or stow them in purpose-built boxes (heavier, but a more secure location). These should be made of a fireproof material.

You probably don't need a trip-meter at this point either, though if it's there, all well and good, so long as you can work out how to handle it. Unless the rally runs into darkness, you probably don't need a map light or a map magnifier, but you will need some sort of map pocket on or near your door, as well as a pencil clip in a handy location. At this stage we're trying to keep things as simple as possible, so I don't want to clutter you or your 'office' with too much kit.

Overalls of a fire-resistant nature are now a legal

Above left *Some sort of door pocket is essential for maps and oddments, plus clips for pens and pencils.* (Lodge.)

Left *Basic flame-resistant overalls are available at moderate cost.* (Lodge.)

requirement for special stage events. You should feel strongly about fire protection, so find yourself a set of overalls from the specialist shop where you got the helmet. Prices can be quite reasonable but, as with most things, the more you pay, the better the quality. Note there is a difference between 'fire-resistant' and 'fireproof'. Safety, comfort and practicality are the prerequisites. They shouldn't be so tight-fitting as to restrict movement, otherwise an activity such as changing a spare wheel mid-stage will be a painful experience. At some point you are going to be glad you got them, and what the hell—they look wonderful! So now we've got the essentials together, shall we get on with the rallying?

Chapter 4

Going rallying

I f everything has gone to plan so far, you should by now have received an acknowledgement of your entry from the organizers (which is not a guarantee of a starting place), followed by an acceptance. It may be however that despite doing everything right on the entry form, you'll only be placed on the reserve list and not guaranteed a start at this stage. A polite (I stress the word) call or visit to the entries secretary may give you some idea of your chances of starting. Though you may be disappointed at being a reserve, abuse and strong language will get you precisely nowhere, but a calm, reasoned discussion may very well bring rewards.

Out of those, say, 100 entries, you can guarantee that at least 5 per cent will not start; reasons? They crashed the car last week, they're stuck for bits, they've run out of money, there's a bereavement in the family, their wives won't let them out to play. Even if you're a seemingly hopeless 10th reserve, don't despair. Some of those reserves will withdraw just because they've not been put on the entry list, some may be in the reserves because they didn't send a cheque (they are the ones least likely to appear), so with a bit of luck and persistence, you'll get a start.

Countdown to the rally

Unless you're mechanically inclined, you might not have had too much to do with the preparation of the rally car. No reason why a co-driver shouldn't be mechanically inclined of course—I know several good ones who are—but generally such matters are more in the driver's province. However, now would be a good time to check that all is well in the preparation department. How often I have seen potentially good crews come unstuck through rushed, last-minute mechanical fettling. Even if you're not of a mechanical bent, there are bound to be some jobs you can do, if only cleaning the car or applying decals, to help the effort along. Assuming the car is mobile at this stage, it would be a good idea to have a test run out together, just to see that everything is working properly and that there's nothing obviously wrong or out of place. I'm not suggesting a law-breaking full out attack on the public highways, but an open, deserted bit of road with good visibility should be useful, so long as you're sensible. Night time, when the roads are quiet, would be a good time, as well as giving you the chance to set the spotlights, if darkness is envisaged on your event. If you know someone with a bit of not-too-rough farm track, that would be even better, but such gems are hard to find. It would make sense to check out the location of various items, like fire extinguisher, master switch, fuses, jack, wheelbrace; in fact a practice wheel change, so that you (a) know how the jack works and (b) can work out who does what, wouldn't go amiss at this point.

Final instructions

Assuming these are in your possession, then a good, careful read would be a good idea. There may be some important matters contained therein, like an additional map required, or an extra award for which you're eligible. Of particular interest are any changes to the timing arrangements—the amount of maximum lateness and between which controls it will apply, what lateness penalties will be applied, and so on. There may be some, or indeed all, of the route and service information. Obviously, plot out whatever you've been given, but let's assume for now that the main route information will be given at the signing-on. Organizers of smaller events tend to do it that way, either because they aren't able to finalize their stage routes until quite late, or because they wish to deter the unscrupulous from going to have a pre-event look.

There may be some matters of technical significance for the driver—some particular aspect which the scrutineer has announced he's going to examine this week. If so, make sure that your driver is aware of it. The driver should also have an RAC MSA Rally Log Book for the car; this is done so that scrutineers can keep a check on 'rogue' cars, or on jobs which were promised to be done on the last rally. If he hasn't got one, make an appointment to have the car checked by your local RAC MSA scrutineer as soon as possible.

You'll also get the entry list, with your start number shown. Make sure the details on the entry list are correct—names, car, capacity, class, awards eligibility; if not, call the entries secretary, with whom you should now be on first name terms.

All that remains now is to agree the travel arrangements for the big day with your driver—who's collecting whom, when and where—and you're about set. Well, almost.

Service crew

It sometimes amazes me that a motor car which has had far more care and attention lavished upon it than the average family banger is unable to survive a day's gentle rallying without the attentions of a service crew. Your driver may well have come to the same conclusion and already decided that funds being what they are and the preparation of the car being so excellent, etc., etc., you will be tackling this epic without the benefit of a service crew. On many smaller events, this is perfectly feasible: a full tank of petrol will last you the day, as will the tyres; you've got tools on board and can turn your hands to most mechanical duties, so why bother?

The answer is that it may be difficult to avoid getting a service crew. Motor clubs seem to abound with people just dying to do this seemingly uninspiring task, and if friends have helped with the preparation even in a minor way, you can be sure they would just love to come out and service for you. While you might not actually need them, they can be quite useful, even if it's only to clean the screen, tip in a bit of petrol and swop the tyres round. (Perhaps some agreement as to who will do what will save some confusion on the day.) This saves you getting your hands dirty (a good idea for a co-driver) and makes for good moral support, which you will probably need at some point in the day. Quite often, it won't cost you anything; these people will come just for the thrill of it. Strange breed of people, these service crews.

Scrutineering

This is an important part of proceedings and you must try to get it right. Firstly, make sure you and your driver have all the correct documents—Club Licences, Competition Licences (including Entrants and Advertising Permits where required), road licences, insurance (Bowring or normal cover endorsed for the rally), car log book, rally log book (RACMSA requirement), MOT certificate, current tax disc on the car. If the organizers don't provide numbers, make sure you have two sets of the correct figures, plus a white background. Sod's Law says it will be wet and windy if you apply these at scrutineering,

Above right *Applying rally plates, numbers and decals is best done indoors, where rain and wind will not affect the application.* (Lodge.)

Top left *Noise check in progress before the event.* (Lodge.)

Above left *Scrutineering is an important preliminary. Note the helmets on the roof, ready for inspection.* (Lodge.)

so do it beforehand if you can (you can always cover up the numbers for the trip to scrutineering). A set of badly applied decals is an unsightly mess.

The final instructions will state where and when the car must be scrutineered, either a specific time or between certain times. Invariably there's a queue, and as it can be a rather stressful time all round, I recommend that you turn up in plenty of time and get the whole business out of the way as early as possible. Even if you're ahead of your 'slot' time, there's usually a gap which the scrutineers are happy to fill with another 'customer'.

First of all you'll have to go through the noise check. This is the hurdle at which several runners fall, but if your car is

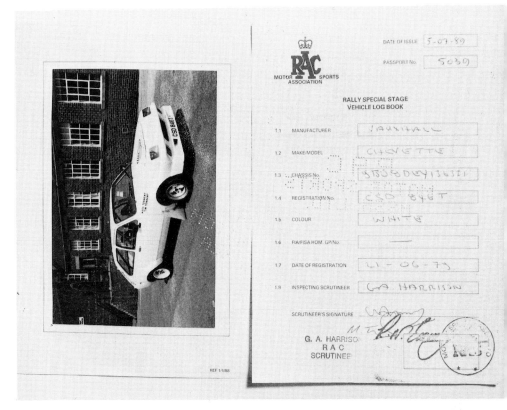

Above *For non-International events, your rally car will need an RAC MSA Rally Log Book.*

Right *Make sure you have all your paperwork to hand for signing on and remember to check for any last-minute amendments.* (Lodge.)

properly prepared, there should be no problem.

Scrutineering itself can also trip up a few, if only because there are so many ways of failing it. While you're waiting in the queue, wander up to the scrutineering bay and watch the scrutineers at work. Quite often they will pick on a particular area (clearly they cannot examine every aspect of every car), and perhaps from your 'recce' you can spot what this is, though if you too are the wrong side of the regs on this point, it's maybe rather late to do much about it. But do understand the scrutineer's task: it's not to throw everybody out of the rally, but to see that the rules are applied fairly and to see that safety (including your safety) is paramount. That's quite a responsibility, and even if he seems a rather crusty old gent, understand that the 'scrute' is probably quite knowledgeable and experienced, and that he has your best interests at heart. If you do run into problems here, always remember to remain courteous and reasonable. If you do, the 'scrute' will probably suggest ways to correct the deficiency and assuming that correction is within your power, he'll probably pass you on re-submission.

Next stop should be the signing on room, sometimes in the same place, sometimes elsewhere. Here's where you will need to produce most if not all of the documents listed previously. This is a moment when drivers have a tendency to wander off, because when momentarily separated from their wheels, and with boring paperwork in the offing, they take the opportunity to have conversations with mates, swop stories about the last rally or chat up the nearest bit of talent—just when you need them to sign the official sheet. Sometimes I feel one of those long, retractable dog leads would be useful for such occasions. So, try to have him stay at least within calling distance. Keep an eye open for the official notice board; sometimes there's nothing of real note on it, but occasionally there's a

To make the best use of limited stage mileage, many smaller events use split junctions. Be sure to understand what is intended. (Lodge.)

route amendment or timing change. Normally you should receive this in the form of a written bulletin, but that doesn't always happen on small events, so make sure you check the notice board. In signing on, you may also be signing to say that you've seen the amendment(s), and if you haven't seen them, you could be heading for problems later.

Having successfully negotiated this area, you'll be given your route information and time cards (check all are complete) and you're now free to go and make your final preparations for the rally.

Navigation

If it's a single venue rally (also known as a 'multi-use stage rally'), the navigation will be very easy. Find yourself a quiet spot and read through everything carefully. Quite often the 'road book' will come in map or plan form. Hopefully, it should be easy enough to understand, but just to be sure, it's a good idea to go and have a chat with a co-driver higher up the order, to see if his understanding of various points is the same as yours. There'll be a stated time at which you should present the car at the start, so once you've established that, make sure the team knows—driver and service crew. They can then look after the final preparations while you make yours. Take a good look at the time cards, note which 'box' should be filled in by which set of marshals—time control, stage start, stage finish, etc. Sometimes you will need to fill in your own competition number in a box for identification purposes. Sometimes that is already printed on. There may be a passage control for card collection, so that the results team can process the scores. Servicing will generally be fairly free, but just check if it's a timed service, with time controls before and after.

Walk the course

In the case of a single-venue event, it may be possible to walk the course. Perhaps you should check with a senior marshal before you do, because strictly speaking it's not within the regulations. If it's acceptable, suggest that the driver takes a stroll with you, well before the action takes place; you can both learn something from this, as well as easing the pre-rally tensions with a bit of exercise. The driver should be looking for the right line through a corner or sequence; you'll be looking for places that can catch out either the driver or yourself.

Quite often with single-venue events the organizers have only limited stage mileage to use, so to get the most out of it they use 'split junctions', that is, places where rally cars starting the stage join the main route and where those finishing the stage leave the main route. The former can be a bit tricky when there's an existing competitor boring down on the junction, but usually it will be well marshalled and with some sort of funnelling system to merge the two (or more) competitors. The latter can be trickier still, because in the heat of the moment it's easy to take the wrong 'slot' and either go out of the stage prematurely or do an extra lap before finishing. Both are highly undesirable, because they will net you a 'maximum' score/exclusion or an unnecessarily long stage time respectively, so you must make sure that you and your driver know exactly what to do at what point. By the way, if you do make either of the aforesaid mistakes, what you must not do is stop and reverse or try to regain the correct route; that's dangerous and you will rightly be excluded.

It's fair to say that the single biggest cause of problems on these smaller events is the split junction situation, so you should pay extra attention to its intricacies. What may be an easy section on the first pass may well turn out to be extremely tricky on the second, with a tight turn-off demanding an entirely different approach speed and line. The proximity of other cars, effectively taking a different route at the same point, may also complicate matters. Inevitably, because many single-venue rallies take place on airfields, the organizers install chicanes to bring the speed down. These too need some thought as to the speed and line, if you are not to get caught out by the somewhat artificial features.

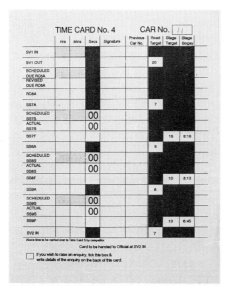

Left *The design of time cards varies considerably. Check which box should be filled in at which point.*

Below *The marshals' clock—nice and clear to read—with the 'hold' button on the right. (Lodge.)*

Learning from others

By now, the early numbers will have started, so see how they set about tackling the stage. Apart from being entertaining to watch, note how they approach the bits you earmarked as tricky during your 'walkabout'. Also note the place where they seem to be having problems, which may be quite different from where you thought the difficulties would be. If you've time, go and talk to someone who's finished the stage. He'll usually tell you about any tricky places, like where a lot of mud has been thrown onto a corner by earlier cars. Also if there's time, see how the time control is working—where the marshal is filling in the cards—and how the stage start procedure is operating.

The moment of truth

Soon, however, the moment of truth will arrive, so now's the time to get installed in the car, ready for action. So helmets ready—you don't need them on just yet—time card, road book, watch? All ready, so let's move on down to the start, giving us about 5 to 10 minutes to wait outside the control. There'll be a bit of shuffling to get you all in the right order—that should be obvious by the door numbers. If there's a queue which is unlikely to clear before your due time, get out and find the marshal (he may be wandering up and down the queue, looking harrassed) and ask him, nay insist, on your specific time. Don't wait for him to find you—he won't necessarily do so, in which case you may incur unneccessary lateness. You can put helmets on about a couple of minutes before you're due in, and when your time comes up, move into the control.

On these events there's not too much ceremony with FISA-type boards or going in one minute before due time or three-minute 'belting up' time (we'll cover that later), just ensure that you're on 'your' minute, hand your card over and ask for that minute. Check the marshal has written it legibly and correctly (if he hasn't, politely suggest that he does and get him to initial any correction). Then move on down to the start line. Ensure that the driver doesn't pull up too close behind the car in front—even on tarmac, loose stones can be thrown up and crack your screen or lamps. If the cars are starting at one-minute intervals, the start procedure is quite straight-forward; many single-venue events use 30-second intervals, which is quite a bit tighter. This situation is covered in Chapter 5.

When it's your turn, get the time card inscribed with the

Above left *Checking into the time control. See the marshal puts the correct time in the correct place and initials his entry. (Lodge.)*

Top right *At the stage start, don't allow your driver to pull up too close to the car on the start line—stones can fly up and damage your windscreen or lights. (Lodge.)*

Above right *Helmets on, belts tight and zero your stop-watch ready for the stage start. (Kolczak.)*

Below *Countdown. The marshal calls out 5—4—3—2—1, sometimes using hand signals in addition. (Lodge.)*

GO—a good countdown technique via the co-driver should prevent a jump start. (Lodge.)

time, check that this will coincide with the correct start time on the marshal's clock, then stow the time card—and don't forget where you put it. If after this point in time there's a 'hold' (there may have been an accident on the stage), make sure the marshal gives you a new time and initials the correction. Otherwise, tighten belts (no doubt for the umpteenth time), have the road book or plan ready, plus a pencil, and the stop-watch zeroed. I prefer to have my window closed to eliminate wind roar and exhaust noises, but some crews like to have a bit of ventilation this way. On a dusty stage, an open window might draw dust inside the car, so take care. If you need to 'hang on' for support, you should never, ever put your hand through the open window to hold onto the door frame. If the car rolls, your hand will suffer serious injuries. Similarly, don't hold the roll-cage, which can trap your hand in the event of an inversion. A grab-handle on the door or upper roll-cage should suffice, if you feel you need it, but in my experience your hands will be full of road book/map/pace notes. A good countdown technique is essential to reduce the driver's natural tendency to jump the start in his anxiety to get away quickly. On the countdown call each point to the driver: '30', '15', '10', and for the last five, actually watch the marshal mouthing the words and count down out loud in synch with him: '5—4—3—2—1—GO'. Remember to start your stop-watch on 'GO'.

Now, follow the road book/plan, but don't try to tell your driver too much, you'll just confuse him. Just highlight the tricky points—the entry split junction, a chicane perhaps, a tricky place you spotted in the walk or where someone told you there was mud on the road, and finally the exit junction and the flying finish board. On a confusing junction, you may have to point at the direction you want him to take. All these things may seem very obvious to you, but when he's concentrating on

Below left *Flying finish. One marshal stops the clock, the other records the time on his check sheet. (Kolczak.)*

Below right *At the stop line the marshal records the time from the flying finish, with his own clock as a back-up. The time card on a clipboard is a good idea, but note that the next car is already arriving — time to leave. (Kolczak.)*

Bottom right *Now you can go to the service area. (Lodge.)*

driving as hard as he can go the driver will develop 'tunnel vision', and not necessarily notice things which are quite apparent to the co-driver. Use the pencil to mark any unexpectedly dodgy places (for next time), or to keep your place. You'll probably have to hold tight onto the road book so that it doesn't fly off your lap.

As you cross the flying finish, stop the stop-watch, check the time, congratulate the driver if he's driven well (they like to have their egos inflated, you know) and get him to pull up by the stop board. If he overshoots this, he must not reverse back to the control—you have to get out and walk back. Note that as well as recording the time on your card, the marshals will also write your time on their own check sheet; this is used for checking discrepancies later. The driver's work may be over for now, but yours certainly is not. Again see that your time coincides with the marshal's time. Ask to see the clock anyway—it should be readily available. Query the time if it's more than five seconds slower (not if faster) than your time. Check that the marshal hasn't made any writing errors and move on promptly. There may be someone else bearing down on the stop line. Now you may be allowed to work on the car, in which case once you've booked into service (if necessary) you can take your helmet off and relax; your first special stage is over. Check when you're due to report for the next stage (there could be a longish wait) and supervise any repairs or adjustments to the car.

Below left *Some plotting to do. It helps if someone can read out the references.* (Lodge.)

Below right *Consistency in your map-marking is desirable. Stickers are used for service points.* (© *Crown copyright.*)

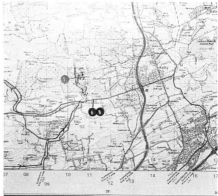

Multi-venue

While many things are the same for a multi-venue rally, there are some significant differences. Firstly, the scrutineering, start and first special stage may not be in the same general area, so in that case you won't get the benefit of a 'walkabout'. Secondly, you'll have a bit more plotting to do. The road book may be supplied as a set of map references for you to plot; you should now be able to handle these, but if the driver or someone from the service crew can read the references out to you, it will speed things up as well as give you another pair of eyes to look at any areas of difficulty in the paperwork. I tend to mark maps with a single line along the left hand side of the road, with a single dash across the road to show the location of a control.

It doesn't really matter how you mark your maps, so long as it's clear to you and it's consistent. Some events may specify a particular direction of approach, for example 'NNE'. This means you must arrive at that point from the North North East and any other direction could give you a penalty for wrong direction of approach.

Tulips

On the other hand, the road book may be presented to you as a set of 'tulip' diagrams, so called from the old Tulip Rally in Holland which pioneered the method. Though these may look like hieroglyphics, they're really quite simple. Look on them as a picture of the junction, seen from overhead. The ball is the direction from which the rally route comes, the arrow the direction to which the rally route goes.

You will need to develop some way of communicating this information to your driver. 'Fork right' or 'Turn left at T' are straightforward enough, as is 'Take the next turn right'; however, 'Straight at cross roads' can be nerve-wracking if you don't remind him about the Stop or Give Way sign, while 'Straight on at roundabout' has been known to be taken literally, with the driver going over the top of the grassy mound. Better to say 'Roundabout, take second exit'. Sometimes, on complicated junctions you will need to point at the road you want. Unless you are precise about where you want the driver to go, you will find yourself in embarrassing situations which, though probably not your fault, will seem that way to others, so try to get a good, consistent basis for your instructions. Again you will have to keep a good hold on your road book, because even on the road sections a stiffly sprung rally car (or a harsh driver) will tend to dislodge it from your grip unless you are wary.

In the left hand column are the distances, one the cumulative total distances from one time control to the next, the other the interval distances between each junction. You will need to give your driver some sort of distance when approaching a junction, so that he knows in which general area he's supposed to look for the occasionally obscure 'slot'. Though your road book will be in decimals of a mile, your driver will probably relate more to a distance in yards. Since one tenth of a mile is 176 yards, you will need to get used to doing some rapid mental calculations on a regular basis. Of course, in kilometres this is much easier. On the right-hand side are the countdown distances to the next time control. The other bits and pieces can usually be deciphered from the key in the front of the road book, but generally they're fairly obvious. Of particular interest are the markings for 'service forbidden' and gravel/tarmac.

The distances are meant to be used in conjunction with a trip-meter, but don't worry if you don't have one. You can still transfer the information onto the maps. Some people, I hesitate to class them as true co-drivers, don't bother to plot out the maps if they have this type of road book. Well, what if the trip-meter breaks down (a not unusual occurrence), or if the road book is wrong (also a good possibility), or if you make a navigational error (surely not), or if the road is blocked and you have to find a way round? Without the route on the maps, you've little chance of sorting out the problem. So, always plot out the route and keep the maps handy in the car so that you can keep your place on the road sections. If you don't have a trip-meter, work off the maps all the time, but be sure you've put everything on them and haven't missed out a passage control or some other significant information.

A 'tulip' style road book.

Thirdly, you'll need to do a bit more accurate timekeeping. Presenting the car at the start will be pretty much the same, but then you'll probably have a timed section to stage one. Remember what we said in Chapter 2 about time. The important thing is to make sure you don't check in early, nor unnecessarily late. Quite often a time card will give you a space for calculating your due time; simply add the minutes allowed for the section to your start time to give you your due time at the time control; then all you need to do is to see that your driver maintains a reasonable speed en route. No point in going quickly—the time allowance should be easy anyway—but keep an eye on progress. A speed of 30 mph (the maximum for a non-motorway road section) is a mile every two minutes, so it's easy to see if you're up or down on time. Let the driver know either way, so that he can adjust his road pace accordingly. One point: the police often decide to set up speed traps on sections of the rally route. You have been warned.

Target timing

Checking in at stage one will be the same as our single venue: arrive at the time control at the correct time, go through the formalities and move down to the start. Again, it is the same procedure as before. At the finish, things become a little more involved, because if the rally is run on Target Timing (as most British rallies are), the time at which you finish the special stage (discounting the seconds) is also the time at which you start the next road section. So the marshal must first record the finish time (check he's got it right) and then record the hours and minutes as the 'out' time from the control. Check also that these correspond. You then have the minutes of the next road section to achieve the following time control on time. If it's only a short section, leading to another stage, you might as well keep your helmets on. Once again, even though you may be under pressure, make sure you don't book in early. The motto should be check, check, check all the time. We're all human and can make mistakes; that's more likely to happen when we're under pressure and doing stages in quick succession, even more so if thing start to go wrong. But we'll deal with problems in Chapter 10.

Passage controls

In order to process the results, the organizers need to collect times from you at regular intervals, so you will need to surrender time cards at selected points, which should be shown in the road book. It doesn't matter what time you enter a passage control, the marshals won't be recording a time. However, they must take the relevant card (make sure they don't take the wrong one) and give you a signature as proof that they've done that. They may also need to transfer a time from the end of the last card to the start of the next. Again, always see that it's done correctly. It's as well to keep a record of all your times, not just on the stages, but at each time control. Jot them down in the road book and then you've got a record in case of discrepancies at the finish, because with the time cards removed, you lose that particular piece of evidence.

If for some reason you are dropping time, you also need to keep a check of how much so that you don't go over maximum lateness. If you don't keep a tally of time dropped, you may not realize you've been excluded until the official results come up. Remember also that no amount of lateness can be recovered by booking in early.

Main controls

Sometimes, around the lunch halt period or even late in the event, the organizers might put in a Main Control. At these, instead of using a Target Time from the previous control, you are required to present the car at a Scheduled Time. While lateness penalties at other controls may be non-existent apart from maximum lateness, quite often lateness at a Main Control carries severe penalties, like one minute per minute late. It's a bit like the start, at which there are usually heavier penalties for being late than on a normal road section. The rally entry may have got a bit spread out, due to retirements or delays, so the Main Control is used to regroup competitors and put them back at one-minute intervals. This is good for safety reasons, but there are several pitfalls, depending on how the organizers operate these controls. Knowledge of the lateness penalties and maximum lateness rules is essential. Once again, it pays to study the regulations and final instructions closely, so that you can make sure you, and the rest of the team know the restart time, and get it right.

Keeping the score

You may feel that you've got your hands full enough already, but you should also keep a score sheet of all your stage times, together with a running total. This is not only to check on the organizer's tally, which we covered two paragraphs back, but also to check on your progress relative to other competitors,

STAGE TIME RECORDS

Competition Number	1	2	3	4	5	6	7	8		10	12	13	14	15	16
Driver	MW	OC	JIM	COLIN	FRANCO	RUSSOC	MARK	SERGE		KENNY	SWYN	WULF	HAKAN	DAVEM	AMBRW
Brought Forward	FORD	TOY	AUDI	FORD	FORD	FORD	VW	TOY		FORD	FORD	AUDI	PEUG	VAUX	FORD
Stage 1 / 5 2 — Total	5-02	4-52	5-05	5-05	5-03	5-09	5-27	5-13		5-26	5-11	5-05	5-18		5-07
Stage 2 / 4 6 — Total	4-54	4-38	4-56	4-49	4-52	4-50	5-13	5-01		5-03	4-54	4-55			4-57
— Total	9-56	9-30	10-01	9-54	9-55	9-59	10-40	10-16		10-29	10-05	10-00			10-04
Stage 3 / 2 0 — Total	1-57	1-53	2-02	1-57	2-11	2-03	2-09	2-01			2-01	2-04			2-03
— Total	11-53	11-23	12-03	11-51	12-06	12-02	12-49	12-15			12-06	12-04			12-07
Stage 4 / 5 2 — Total	6-12	5-35	5-51	5-67	5-46	5-49	6-18	6-02			5-55	5-54			5-56
— Total	18-05	16-58	17-54	17-38	17-52	17-51	19-07	18-17			18-01	17-58			18-04
Stage 5 / 6 4 — Total	6-30	6-26	6-46	6-36	6-34	6-33	7-17	6-65							
— Total	24-35	23-24	24-40	24-14	24-26	24-24	26-24	25-02							
Stage 6 / 3 1 — Total	3-45	3-39	3-50	3-49	3-51	3-50		3-58							
— Total	28-20	27-03	28-30	28-03	28-17	28-14									
Stage 7 / 2 0 — Total	13-69	13-36	14-42	13-51	13-59	14-00		14-34				16-23			
— Total	42-09	40-39	43-12	41-54	42-16	42-14									
Stage 8 / 3 9 — Total C/F	4-06	4-02	4-15	4-09	4-10	4-12		4-22							
Total C/F	46-15	44-41	47-27	46-03	46-26	46-25		48-01							

Above *Keeping the score is an integral part of a co-driver's duties. Here is a typical score sheet.*

Left *A co-driver totals up his stage times. Be happy in your work.* (Lodge.)

Below *Prizes for club rallying are generally modest.* (Lodge.)

both overall and in your class, as well as fellow club members with whom you might be having a bit of a dice. There's no point in having a competition if you don't know where you're lying in that competition. Don't be tempted to give out false times to, or withold times from your rivals, otherwise you'll soon acquire a reputation as a spoilsport and your tactics might be practised on you.

The finish

At the end of the day you should have a total which corresponds with the organizer's total. Check the official results on the score-board and speak to one of the officials if there are any discrepancies. On smaller events the results are produced manually, perhaps on a big score-sheet, or on strips hung on a line, though computerized results are becoming more widespread and can produce more comprehensive information. Hopefully you won't be involved in any protests on your first outing.

Once the job of computation is out of the way, you can relax and enjoy the post-rally discussion amongst your own team and with your friends and rivals until the results go 'final'. This can be a pleasant time of rallying, as tales are swopped with ever-increasing exaggeration of the adventures encountered in the day's sport. It's a useful time too because you can learn things from the more experienced crews as well as make contacts which might well be useful in the future. Rallying is a very convivial sport and the get-together after the event is often one of the highlights.

Once the prizegiving is over, you'll head for home, but it's a good idea to fix up a meeting with your driver—say, at the next club-night—to settle matters financial, discuss the rally, analyse what went well and what went wrong, as well as plan your next outing. Next outing? Will there be one? Did you enjoy this one? The chances are that you did, very much so. After all, this is a day you'll probably remember all your life, your first special stage rally. If all has gone well it should have whetted your appetite for a bit of forestry rallying.

Chapter 5

Into the woods

The backbone of British special stage rallying has always been the forestry roads. When the RAC Rally started to use these tracks in the 1960s as an alternative to the rather artificial driving tests which had previously decided the event, it started a trend which has had a profound influence on rallying. In their wisdom, the builders of these roads constructed them primarily so that large forestry vehicles could extract timber in most weathers without excessive difficulty. Consequently, the roads are generally very well founded and are usually not too tight, nor the gradients too steep. This means that the surface, albeit loose, holds together reasonably well and the tracks are fast, flowing and suitable for rallying.

Following the RAC's lead, other British Internationals took to the forests, followed by Nationals and even Restricted events. So by the 1970s, even club drivers could cut their teeth on a small forestry event. Of course, there was a price to pay and that price escalated (and continues to do so) at an alarming rate. The Forestry Commission seeks to recover the cost of repairing the roads after a rally has been through (which is fair enough); how they gauge that cost, and how much repair work is done after the passage of a rally, is open to question at times. Nevertheless, the end result for the competitor is that he must expect to pay ever more in entry fees for the privilege of rallying on some of the finest loose-surfaced tracks in the world. Let us hope that the price doesn't become so great that no one except factory teams can afford to pay it.

Anyway, enough of the politics; apart from greater entry fees, let's see what else is involved in going forest rallying. Depending on where you live, you may need to travel a good deal further than you did to get to your local single-venue event. So much so that you might need to consider overnight

Above *UK forestry roads come in various guises: flat...* (Lodge.)

Top right *...hilly...* (Kolczak.)

Above right *...wide...* (Lodge.)

Right *...or narrow.* (Lodge.)

accommodation; obviously, neither you nor your driver will deliver of your best if you've driven all through the night to get there. Perhaps one of you has friends or relatives in the area who can put you up for the night, but a local bed & breakfast hotel won't be too expensive, so this shouldn't be a big obstacle. Quite often, the event organizers can find such accommodation for you if you ask them early enough.

Car preparation becomes more important for the forests and your driver should take specialist advice on this. Underbody protection and suitable tyres are certainly important, but let's concentrate on the co-driver's angle.

The seat

The rougher nature of the roads and the more sideways attitude of the car will definitely expose any inadequacies in your seating arrangements, so you really should obtain a proper competition seat. If the car hasn't got one already, try to persuade your driver that he should invest in one. The usual requirements apply to its correct installation, but you will

Below left *A foot brace is useful. Note the foot-operated buttons for horn and trip-meter. (Lodge.)*

Below right *There are many kinds of trip-meter. This is the old, mechanical Halda. (Lodge.)*

probably find a foot brace quite useful. I mention this, not because I think you're going to be scared out of your wits and need to brace yourself at every corner, but because to do a good job you need to be well located. If your feet are not firmly placed, they tend to move about, making you feel insecure and distracting the driver. Quite often, the car's floor or front bulkhead is not at the right distance nor at the right angle to achieve the ideal location for your feet, but the foot-plate can be set to be just right for you. It's also useful for fitting the co-driver-operated horn button (see Chapter 3), because on a forestry event you're likely to have your hands full (in more ways than one), and you can activate it with the deft movement of a foot. However, make sure this button is not in a place where you'll catch it every time you get in and out of the car—it's embarrassing to keep blowing the horn on such occasions.

Trip-meter

Talking of buttons, the foot-brace is also a good place to mount a foot-operated zero button for the trip-meter, some distance away from the horn button so that it can be operated by the other foot. This is the first time I have mentioned this, but on a forestry rally you're going to find a trip-meter very useful at times, so now's the time to get one sorted out if the driver's funds will allow. If not, then you can indeed manage to

Right *Halda's electronic successor.* (Lodge.)

do such rallies without, although at a disadvantage.

In the past, the mechanically driven Halda was an almost universal fitting. It was solid, generally reliable and easy to operate. You will still find quite a few of these around, fitted to older rally cars. The drawback to this instrument was that its cable drive (from wheel or transmission) was vulnerable to all manner of ills, including poor installation, underbody stone damage and poor maintenance. Its other failing was that to recalibrate it, you had to extract the gearing carriage and replace it with another set of gears—that is, if you knew which other gears you needed. It was quite fiddly, and you could not always achieve the calibration you required. Co-drivers' bags tended to be weighed down with calibration charts, spare gears and the tools for changing them. If your rally car is elderly and has such an instrument keep it—it'll soon be a collector's item—but make sure you get it properly serviced before the rally. This means finding a measured mile somewhere, driving over it and seeing whether your reading is over or under by a significant amount. If so, you should follow the maker's instructions for recalibration.

In the same way that the digital watch has improved timing standards, so has the new generation of electronic trip-meters improved the lot of co-drivers. Recalibration is generally a matter of twiddling a few bezels and can be easily done while on the move if necessary. Installation is simpler, because the vulnerable drive cable has been replaced by a probe (which can pick up a signal from any one of a number of moving parts) and connecting wires. However, this aspect can give problems, so try to make sure that the instrument, and particularly the probe, is installed in accordance with the manufacturer's recommendations. It's no use having the best trip-meter available if it's going to pack up just a couple of miles into the event.

Which is the best one to have? I'm afraid I couldn't begin to advise you, because fashions change so rapidly in this area. Just as one 'meter seems to have achieved the highest reputation, along comes another with supposedly better features. Halda produced an electronic version of their mechanical wonder, but not everyone found this easy to read or operate. The Terratrip found favour in the UK with quite a lot of co-drivers, but the choice has expanded rapidly. One word of warning though—as with the digital watches, don't choose one with too many features; you have to be able to use the instrument without too much thought during the rally. You will need a big, bold LED display (in my view this is better than LCD under varying light conditions), with an overall and an interval

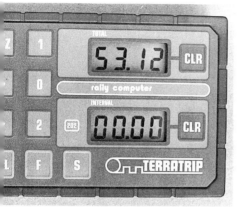

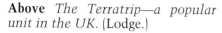

Above *The Terratrip—a popular unit in the UK.* (Lodge.)

Above right *The Coralba (left) with the Rallymaster (right). Belt and braces.* (Hodson/CCC.)

Right *The Brantz. The remote zeroing device should be more positively located.* (Lodge.)

distance, an easy, preferably remote, zeroing system for the interval (this is where our foot-brace-mounted button comes in) and a straightforward calibration system. Useful but not essential extras would be a dimmer for the display (you could be using it at night in which case the daytime strength could distract the driver), a flexible hood to stop reflections on the windscreen, and a reverse switch—useful for those junction overshoots which you reckon you'll never make....

Many works cars carry the Coralba, which has all these features plus countdown in time and distance, fuel contents, and more. Personally, I prefer something a bit more straightforward. In my Open Championship winning years I used a Brantz, a simple reliable meter which had most of the features I needed and in fact was not very expensive. You pays your money and you takes your choice. With all of these instruments, calibration is quite simple; you can even do it on the first road section of the rally if time for calibration before the event is short. Once you've got it right, make a note of the

figure for future reference, but note that if different tyres or final drive ratios are used, you may need a new calibration figure.

Map light

As far as the car is concerned, the only other thing you'll need is a map light. Even though this may be a daylight rally, you could be travelling to it before dawn or, if you're running well down the order, you could be tackling the last stages in darkness. (Remind the driver of this possibility, otherwise you'll be handicapped without spotlights in such circumstances.) The map light should be mounted so that its illumination comes down from above, rather than back from the dash, sideways from the door or up from the transmission tunnel. You need to keep stray light to a minimum, so fixing the lamp to the roof or roll-cage above your shoulder means that it points down onto your lap, which is exactly where you will need the illumination. Make sure the switch is accessible and doesn't foul your helmet as you sit in position, and see that there's a clip to stow the light when it is not in use, otherwise the stalk dangles down and gets in the way when you don't need it. A spare bulb in your bag of co-driver's bits wouldn't be a bad idea either.

Intercom

An intercom may also be useful, primarily because the clatter of stones on the underside of the car and in the wheel arches is

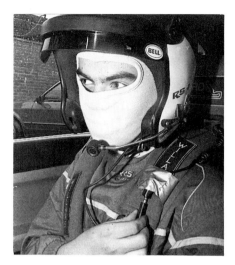

Left *The map light should be mounted high, coming over your shoulder, so that the illumination falls onto your work area. Luigi Pirollo, 1990 RAC Rally.* (Hodson/CCC.)

Above right *The intercom amplifier box should be mounted centrally high, on the roll cage behind your heads.* (Lodge.)

Above left *When correctly taped to the belts, the intercom plugs/ sockets can be connected/disconnected single-handed without looking.* (Lodge.)

obtrusive, though you may find you can manage without it. Once again, there are several to choose from, but the current market leader would appear to be the Peltor, which has built its reputation on being simple and reliable. If you do need to rely on an intercom, the last thing you want is one which packs up mid-stage. In my experience, the more complicated the intercom, the more there is to go wrong. The installation of the ear and mouthpieces is quite critical, from the point of view of effectiveness and comfort, so experiment with the positions before you cement everything in. You should not drill or cut the helmet or its inner shell, as this may compromise the safety of the helmet and possibly render it illegal as far as the scrutineer is concerned.

The amplifier box should normally be mounted centrally on the roll-cage behind your heads; then run the cables along the seat belts and tape the sockets to the part of your straps which holds your upper chest. That way you can find the socket easily by feel and even plug it in one-handed. The plug/socket should part easily for when you leap out of the car, helmet on, having forgotten to disconnect it...

Map reading

I was about to suggest that you set about learning to read the stage route off the map, but on second thoughts, as we're presently concerned with just getting you 'off the ground' with the co-driving, perhaps such a suggestion would be a little ambitious for the relative novice. Really, it depends on your own grasp of maps and confidence in your co-driving.

If you're still feeling your way—for some people, their first rally could be a forest event—then I would advise against trying to read off the map; the workload would be much too high, leading to mistakes, and this could have the effect of putting you off co-driving for good. On the other hand, if you've built up some co-driving experience and already feel comfortable with the maps, then I suggest you turn to Chapter 8, which covers this and other, more specialized, aspects. I must admit, the thought of sending someone not using a map out on forestry does go against the grain, not so much on safety grounds but for the lost opportunity to garner valuable knowledge. However, better that way than to overface you at an early stage. There will be other opportunities.

Final preparations

The RAC MSA doesn't make a different set of rules for forest rallies, so you can expect much of the procedure from our earlier single/multi-venues to be carried over to the forest event. Your pre-event planning and paperwork will also be much the same.

You are more likely to have need of a service crew on this event, because the rally car will have a harder time of it. So persuade your club mates who possess the skills, and preferably the tools and equipment, to come out and service for you. You will need a suitable vehicle for this task; an estate car may suffice, though the ubiquitous Ford Transit is the more usual 'barge'. Your driver may have access to a dedicated service van, which is reasonably well equipped to keep the rally car going throughout the day. Alternatively, you may need to hire a van for this purpose. If so, impress upon your service crew to take care how the heavier items are stowed, because internal damage caused by an insecure trolley jack can soon tarnish your relationship with the friendly local van hire company.

Tyres are a major cost item for rallying, but without encroaching upon the driver's province, may I suggest that you oversee this aspect. Even if to you, tyres are just round and

Above left *Service vans come in all shapes and sizes.* (Hodson/CCC.)

Above right *Round and black. Rally tyres are mostly block-pattern type for forest rallies.* (Lodge.)

black, it will become important later in your co-driving career to understand the complexities of the rubber. So make sure you have a sufficient quantity of a suitable type for the rally in question. Obviously, you won't need the wide, low-aspect ratio racing-type tyres used for an airfield event, unless there's that sort of stage included in the forest rally. Usually a narrower type with a block tread pattern is the norm for forests, but there are endless permutations even to this description. If it's very wet and muddy,the narrower the tyre the better, but then this type of tyre doesn't grip or wear so well if the forest is dry and hard. At this stage in proceedings, your driver will probably have chosen a compromise tyre that will perform adequately in most conditions, without being ideal for the extremes. So for now, just check that someone gets them fitted, balanced, correctly pressured and loaded in the service vehicle.

Depending on your faith in (a) the driver's ability and (b) the car's reliability, you may decide that you don't need a trailer. If the event is not very far away from home, you probably won't, but if it's a long trek to the start, it may be worth considering. You may be able to borrow one or even hire one. Sod's Law says that if you don't take a trailer, that's the time you will need one to bring back the shattered remnants. To be honest, most people now seem to use a trailer to take their car to and from events.

Servicing

This is an area you should now look at more closely. On the single/multi-venue event, servicing was probably centralized and needed little by way of planning. For the forestry event, servicing may again be fairly centralized, but the location or locations may be a bit harder to find. So you will need to spend a bit of time working on the maps of the service crew. Usually the organizers will provide specific service locations, possibly with a dedicated (and perhaps mandatory) route, in advance of the rest of the route information, so take advantage of this and mark up the service crew's maps at an early opportunity.

Perhaps some of your older maps will be adequate, so long as they're not too out-of-date: a new bypass can cause havoc with their navigation. Sometimes the 1:250,000 series maps will suffice; these cover a larger area (so you don't need to buy as many) and generally they are accurate enough for finding service areas. They're also useful to you from a service planning point of view, but we'll look at that later. You don't need to go as far as making a service schedule, but at least brief the service crew on where they have to be and when. Quite often, if a service crew is observed in a forbidden location or off the specified route, there are penalties which may be imposed.

On the event

If you enjoyed the single/multi-venue event, you're almost certain to enjoy the forestry event even more. As I have already pointed out, the event is run to many of the same rules, so the timing procedures I described in Chapter 4 still apply. On the loose, the car in front will throw up more stones on the start line; remember to keep your driver well back at this point.

Assuming you're working off the road book, you will need to use a pencil to cross off each point as you pass it. Each junction/hazard should be numbered, in the road book and on the stage, though don't expect every bad bend or tricky place to be marked by the organizers. Of course, you don't actually have to keep your place, because the stage will be arrowed and the driver should be able to find his way to the finish merely by following the arrows. However, there is a limit to the amount of information a set of arrows can convey; they can also bend in the rain, get knocked down or be 'amended' or removed by spectators, so it pays to keep your place, and this is where the trip-meter is very useful.

Above *The service crew need to be organized to be in the right place at the right time.* (Lodge.)

Right *During the stage, the junctions should be arrowed like this, with a single advance arrow...* (Lodge.)

Below *...followed by two arrows on the junction itself, then by a confirmatory arrow on the correct road.* (Lodge.)

The wrong track will be indicated by this sign. (Lodge.)

Even if the arrows have gone, you still have the tulip diagram of the junction and the trip-meter tells you when you're approaching it. Look through the tulips before tackling the stage and if there are any cautions, dangers (bad jumps, bends with a drop on the outside, etc.) or tricky-looking junctions, make a mental note and work out how you can describe concisely the hazard/junction to your driver mid-stage. It may help to give him a quick briefing and show him the road book (if he understands such things) before clocking into the stage.

Arrowing

The system of arrowing is now fortunately standardized and laid down in the Blue Book. Basically, there should be a single arrow between 50 and 100 metres before the junction, two arrows on the junction to form a 'gate' through which you will pass, and a confirmation arrow after the junction to show you are on the correct road. The incorrect road should have a no-entry sign as well as some sort of physical blockage. The arrows may be angled to show the severity of the junction, but do treat this as an approximation rather than a solid guide.

Because of the cost of using forestry stages on a small event, it's quite likely that the stages may be repeated, at least in part, later in the rally. In this case you should mark down, perhaps obliquely, any troublesome points as you pass the first time. Strictly speaking, this is not legal as this is 'information not supplied by the organizers'.

It may be that the junction/hazard is incorrectly described by the road book or that a jump isn't marked or a corner has become badly rutted. In each case, in the unlikely event of your being quizzed by a marshal, you could argue that your notation was made purely on safety grounds. On the other hand, 'crest at 2.4 miles is flat' is hardly safety information and if caught in possession of such information you could theoretically be penalized for possessing pace notes. Preferably, you'll just have to remember such pearls of wisdom without committing them to paper. The RAC MSA does keep a list of hazards—places with a known history of accidents—and these you are allowed to mark on your maps, though normally the organisers should also mark them in the road book and on the stage itself.

Thirty-second intervals

Another product of the double usage of forestry roads—and this may apply equally to non-forestry events—is 30-second intervals. So far we've operated on the one-minute intervals outlined in the Blue Book, but the double run over a stage may mean that some competitors need to start their second run while later ones begin their first. Clearly, you can't have two cars starting on the same minute, hence the division to 30-second intervals.

So long as the marshals have got the job well organized, it should all work well. If not, or if they're undermanned, it can get a bit chaotic, so be ready for that. Remember, you will have much less time to carry out your pre-start formalities, so get helmets on and belts tight in plenty of time. Warn your driver of the situation, get him to move up to the start line smartly and get the time card filled in promptly, still checking for possible errors. Remember that if you're starting on the half-minute, rather than a whole minute, your finish time seconds as shown by the marshal's clock will also be half a minute adrift, though of course your stop watch will show a normal time.

Above *The firebreak—one of the surprise elements of forestry rallying. Note how the road, as indicated by the tree line, seems to go fairly straight over the crest...* (Lodge.)

Below *...Even seen from the crest, it still seems to lead straight ahead...* (Lodge.)

Bottom *...But now you see that it dives down to the right, with only a track going straight on. And just look at those logs lurking on the apex. A classic forest rallying situation.* (Lodge.)

Firebreaks

One tricky hazard, for which our forests are noted, is the firebreak feature. The forestry planners put these in to try to prevent flames jumping across from one part of the forest to another should there be a forest fire. A road is in itself a firebreak, but there are plenty of places where a firebreak is needed, but not a road. The trouble is, firebreaks give the appearance from a distance of being roads, and are of similar width, so quite often the driver's eye is caught by the line of trees forming the firebreak and he will commit himself to that line, only to discover as he arrives over the crest that the road goes hard right... Fortunately nowadays, most organizers have become alert to such dangers and tape off the gap between the trees in an attempt to persuade you not to go down the firebreak. But they don't always do this, perhaps because they didn't recognize the hazard when they made the road book, or because the forest has changed visually due to forestry workings, so you have to be on the look-out for such possibilities. Almost every co-driver has lurid tales to tell of trips down firebreaks, some terrifying, some amusing, all time-consuming. In time, no doubt you too will be able to add to those tales.

It's all part of the fun and challenge of 'blind' forestry rallying, an experience almost unique to the British Isles. To me, there's something wonderfully thrilling about hurtling down a forest road; it's one of the sport's great experiences, especially when the road is unpractised. I'm sure you'll share that pleasure, but make the most of it: there's no guarantee that we'll have it forever.

Part 2

PROGRESSIVE CO-DRIVING

Chapter 6

Getting serious

So far, we've really only just scratched the surface of the co-driving profession. We've taken short cuts (not literally, I hope), avoided getting equipment wherever possible and not gone into too many of the details. And with good reason: on the assumption that funds are not unlimited, it would be foolish to get tooled up for doing the job seriously if you were unsure of your commitment to co-driving. Similarly, it would be over-ambitious to get too involved in the more specialized intricacies of the craft if that is going to oppress the budding co-driver with complexity and workload.

If you're still with me, and have competed in a selection of the rallies already outlined, then no doubt you will have learned from those experiences and felt that things could be done better in several respects. You would be quite right; though we've covered the bare essentials, there is much, much more to be done to develop your co-driving and hopefully to move up the ladder in terms of driver, car, events and programme. Assuming that you want to progress, now is the time to take stock of your situation and plan out your way ahead.

The driver

You may have secretly entertained the hope that the novice driver you joined up with for your first club rally is going to take you on to National, International and World Championship success. That's not impossible but statistically the chances are something like one in several thousand. In all probability, circumstances are going to get in the way of that initial relationship surviving. If your driver is indeed naturally talented as a rally driver, he should show that talent at a very early stage, whatever the limitations of car or finance. He may not always get the results, but the speed may well be apparent.

Other people will notice that ability and if the luck's really going his way, he might just get the breaks he needs in terms of car and finance. It doesn't often happen in this fairy-tale manner, however. Nevertheless, if he's thrust up the ladder quickly, his backers may feel that, for the protection of their investment, the driver needs a more experienced co-driver, and they're probably quite right. They may be prepared to pay to build his experience, but not yours. Quite often a co-driver of greater experience will bring about the results, simply because he's been down that route before. Clearly, I'm talking about an extreme case here and if you find yourself at the wrong end of it, then your luck's out. In this situation, you're out of a ride, but don't worry, there are plenty of other fish in the sea.

On the other hand, you may find your driver to be of mediocre ability and while you may enjoy his company and the fun of rallying together, you've probably got the feeling that you're not really going places. You may well accept that situation and be happy with it. Not every co-driver wants to progress beyond pure enjoyment of the sport for sport's sake and there's no reason why he should. It may even be that, given time, perseverance and experience, your current driver will indeed progress to the higher echelons. Some are late developers. Only you can decide if that is likely to happen, given the circumstances and whether the probable timescale matches your own ideas of progress. Moving up the ladder will bring about pressures and commitments that you may not be in a position to sustain, for reasons of finance, work or family. No shame in that. However, if you do want to progress more rapidly, in this scenario you may well decide that you need to find yourself a better driver.

Loyalty is a fine attribute, so long as it is rightly placed. However, there is no rule that says you must stick to a certain driver (nor him to you) for a season or whatever, until you are much further along the road to professionalism. You are generally free to take on as many 'rides' as time and work will permit. Indeed, if progress and experience are your initial objectives, I would suggest that you try to do as many rallies as you can, with as many different drivers as you can manage. This will certainly broaden your experience in as short a period as possible and you will see rallying from new angles, both theoretical and actual. You might even wish you'd remained faithful to your original driver. Nevertheless, you will benefit from the experience, as you will get to see different rallies and work in different cars with different teams. You will see good ideas that you might wish to employ elsewhere and see mistakes that you don't wish to see repeated anywhere. A season like this should make you less vulnerable to being 'given the elbow' when you join up with a good driver.

If you do your job reasonably well, you will not only build up your own personal reputation, but make plenty of contacts. Don't be afraid to use those contacts; talk to other drivers who are further up the ladder and tell them that you're available. The seed sown now may not flourish initially, but some of it may bear fruit at a later stage. When I was at university (and frankly I was a relative novice), Jack Tordoff was the 'local hero' in Yorkshire; I asked him to bear me in mind if he should ever need a co-driver. Five years later, he did; we got together and very soon won the Circuit of Ireland outright, a first International win for both of us. So you never know; but if you don't ask, you don't get. Quite often, getting a better ride is a matter of being in the right place at the right time, so there is an element of luck. But sometimes you may have to give your luck a bit of a nudge, otherwise the telephone will never ring.

At some point in time this co-driving promiscuity will have to end, because you will need to settle down to a more regular relationship if you are going to achieve success either on events or in a championship or series. If you're showing promise and not making too many mistakes, the offers will come, believe me, because good co-drivers are scarce and many drivers (the good as well as the not so good) will recognize that a capable regular co-driver may well bring about the success that they seek. When the offers come, you may have some difficulty in selecting which one to take, but in your heart of hearts, you'll probably have a gut feeling about which is the best one from your point of view.

The car

You might feel that the choice of car is purely the driver's domain. However, he might not have fully grasped the implications of running a particular type of car and here's where you come in. Through your now burgeoning knowledge of the sport, you should be able to analyse which is the best car to use to progress further, bearing in mind the available resources. I'll come onto the funding shortly, but assuming that the two of you have some resources, you should look really closely at the car. Is it truly competitive in its class/category, or are you being held up by its lack of competitiveness/reliability? Can that competitiveness or reliability be improved by a new engine, better suspension, transmission or brakes, or perhaps better tyres? Indeed, is it worth spending the money on the present car at all? Perhaps it's getting a bit long in the tooth or is out of homologation. This latter point is only important if you're planning to progress to the National or International arena, but it's well worth considering.

Look carefully at the classes and categories in the various championships on offer, be they Regional, BTRDA, National or Open. Not all of these are run on the same basis, so do a bit of research into the background rules and regulations to see where you might have your best chance of success, within your resources. A good assault on a particular class or category will be more valuable than a spasmodic attempt at overall honours. There's certainly no disgrace in doing a 1300 cc or 1600 cc class or a Production Saloon category, particularly if you perform well. Quite often, you can seriously embarrass those who have much more powerful machinery. The BTRDA Clubmans series has operated several schemes over the years which are intended to give runners lower down the field a better chance to shine than on conventional rallies, so why not give that a look?

Might you be better looking at one of several single-make championships? There are plenty to choose from, ranging from humble Ladas and Skodas to Rovers, Vauxhalls and Peugeots. All have their benefits, from low costs through generous prize funds to even works supported drives for the winners. On the other hand, many manufacturers operate quite lucrative bonus schemes, if not an actual championship of their own; these too should be investigated. So do your research and that way you can help your driver to come to a sensible and logical decision—if there is such a thing in rallying!

The funds

When rallying was simpler and cars were less highly specialized, there used to be a strong argument for choosing an unusual car to rally, because that way you were more likely to get noticed if you performed well. To some extent, the same is true now: if you go well in Britain in something other than the ubiquitous Ford, you will attract attention. However, be careful that you're not drawn into a costly development exercise, soaking up funds which could be put to better purpose in a car which is already sorted. It may be that your hands are tied to some extent—the driver may have business connections with a particular marque, which you are obliged to rally if the wherewithal is to be found.

If I knew the sure-fire way to get sponsorship, I would be a rich man. So I'm afraid I can't tell you how to get a sponsor to part with cash for your rally programme, but I can give you a few pointers.

In my experience, 99.99 per cent of all sponsorship at club/national level is done on a person-to-person basis. Writing to companies, telling them how good you are, how successful you'll be and how their support of you will improve their exposure is, unfortunately, doomed to almost certain failure. Don't forget, you are competing with several different types of promotional media—television, radio, newspapers, hoardings and many others—and it's hard to show, certainly with club rallying, that advertising on a rally car is a more effective method. So however well presented, your letter or sponsorship brochure so easily becomes money down the drain and you can waste an awful lot of time on what eventually turns out to be a wild goose chase.

The key is personal contact. That means knowing the right person in a company, impressing him with not only your collective rallying talents but also your promotional professionalism. If he's an enthusiast for the sport, that will help, but nowadays businessmen have to be a hard-nosed breed if they are to succeed. If they want to survive in their business world, they can't take 'charitable' decisions on sponsorship of your rally car if that will be seen by their directors or shareholders as an ineffective use of the advertising/promotional budget.

I'm sorry if that sounds discouraging, but it's better that you and your driver understand the realities so that you don't waste a lot of time hunting non-existing sponsorship. Of

Russell Brookes successfully developed a small initial sponsorship into a long-running major support package by Andrews Heat for Hire. (Lodge.)

course, sponsorship does take place, even at club level, but much of it can be traced to some personal connection between the driver/co-driver and the company. As the saying goes, it's not a case of what you know, but whom you know. So pursue your personal contacts to the best of your ability, but don't waste your time on the 'cold sell'. It may be that you can drum up a bit of local sponsorship, especially if you can develop a high profile in the local newspaper. The amount may be small but it's a start; who knows, it could in time develop into something bigger.

Motor trade companies are a more likely source of revenue, simply because you can be seen to be using their products, be they cars, tyres, oil or other components. Consequently, some car dealers will support rally programmes, but usually only if you're using a current model of car and deal with them in the course of business. The tyre companies also offer support and bonuses, but as your tyre bill is going to be a major cost item, perhaps the best you can hope for initially is a special competition discount on the tyres. Again, develop personal contacts with the competition department and you may be able to get access to good part-worn tyres at little or no cost if you start to produce results. Oil companies are also a good source. Most of them provide bonus schemes, offering free or reduced-price oil if you carry their decals, while their regional outlets sometimes have budgets for supporting local projects. Your rally team is just as worthy a cause as the local youth orchestra or the annual tennis championships—you just have to persuade the regional manager of that.

I hesitate to suggest that people put themselves in debt to go rallying. The past is littered with those who have over-borrowed to finance their beloved sport and then suffered the consequences. Nevertheless, if capital is a problem rather than the operating costs, that may be overcome: your driver might persuade his bank manager to help out; the rally car can be financed in various ways (hire purchase, leasing,etc.), in which case the driver will have to insure it fully and be sure of his ability to repay; perhaps the company where the driver works might assist in arranging finance. My point is that there is usually a way. If people are determined, and I mean really determined, to go rallying, then they'll find a way. Somehow.

Perhaps you feel that all this is down to the driver and you shouldn't get involved in financial matters. Up to a point that's true—you alone can decide what, if any, financial input you as a co-driver should have. You may be happy effectively to 'buy your ride' through making sponsorship money available, particularly if you feel you've uncovered a new talent. It certainly would strengthen your hand within the relationship, though whether that would be a good thing in the long run for either you or your driver is debatable. You could argue that it's healthier to stay clear of such financial entanglements, and I wouldn't disagree. It all depends on the circumstances and it's your decision if those circumstances warrant your financial involvement or not.

The plan

So, having put together the various resources, found yourself a driver of some ability and pointed him in the direction of the right sort of car, you can now sit down and make your plan. Often I have seen people drift rather aimlessly through a season's rallying, and it makes me wonder if there ever was any sort of planning in the first place. It's no earthly good, having got together your package, however limited, entering widely disparate events, changing from this championship to that championship, dividing your effort and ending up with little of significance at the end. Even if you have had no involvement in the financial side or car choice, you should now be looking to exert some influence over the coming activities.

Let me make one overriding suggestion: whatever you decide to do, do it well. It's far better that you do a lesser programme successfully than a bigger programme unsuccessfully. The same goes for the car: don't go for a car that you don't have the resources to run properly. That way, you'll run out of money mid-season and do your chances of progress no good at all. Far better to go down a notch to a less powerful car that you can afford to run and go out and try to dominate the class, rather than struggle for outright honours against people with much better resources. The name of the game is winning; that is what team managers, trade supporters, sponsors and the media are interested in. Don't make excuses as to why the car broke when you were fourth overall—they are not interested in that at all. Quite often, for the cost of running a high powered car on two or three rallies, you could do a whole season in the Lada Championship and get a lot more rallying experience. That may be an extreme case, but I'm sure you get my meaning. Don't just plan to do some rallies, plan to do them to the best of your resources and ability.

RAC Rally

It becomes almost everybody's ambition to do the RAC Rally. It's the highlight of the UK season, the final round of the World

Every crew's ambition is to compete on the RAC Rally. It's a great competition and very well publicized. Carlos Sainz/Luis Moya, 1990. (Kolczak.)

Championship and a wonderful showcase for rallying. It's natural that you and your driver will consider doing it at some point, but be warned—it can be very expensive. I know of some drivers who only do one rally a year—the RAC. But that's a rather extreme way of using your budget, and you'd hardly be in match practice for such an important event. However, it is possible to do the RAC reasonably well without a massive budget and the rewards for winning your class or whatever can be quite high in terms of prize money and trade bonuses.

Whatever your programme, set out with a realistic objective in mind and work hard to attain that objective. It's so much easier to generate publicity on the back of success than on the back of failure, however 'unlucky' the cause or spectacular the accident; consequently, you may be able to tie up a bit of extra sponsorship during the season that will perhaps pay for an overseas trip later in the year, or help you to move up to a more powerful car the following season. Too many people in rallying try to run before they can walk; consequently, a lot of talent goes to waste because of poor planning and management. This is where you come in not only as co-driver but also as mentor and guide; steering your driver in the right direction could just be the best bit of 'navigation' you ever did.

The organization

Having got this far, you need to plan out your programme and get the team organized. The first should not be so difficult, the second could be harder. If it's a particular series or championship, both you and your driver may need to register for it. So, apply to the organizer, sometimes called the co-ordinator, for the necessary paperwork at the earliest opportunity. Sometimes you will have to join a particular club, for example the BTRDA, which being a nation-wide rallying club gets invited to many events; or you might need to be a member of a club within a certain area to qualify. There will probably be a championship entry fee to pay as well. While you may have seen a schedule of events already, the dates of rallies have a nasty habit of being changed and if you're on the list of registered entrants, you should get to hear about any changes quite soon. This could be quite important, because if you discover that one of your events has moved to a date which clashes with the family holiday your wife has just booked, you will have a rather difficult decision to make come the summer....

I would suggest you put the various dates on some sort of chart that you can photocopy and distribute to your driver, service crew, sponsors (if any) and other interested parties. That way, everyone can probably organize their lives around your rally programme. Alternatively, if you end up with some major clashes and/or domestic arguments, perhaps you will have to rethink your programme.

Whatever, it's best to do it at an early stage. Make sure you keep a record of all your results and make a list of the championship points after each round. The motor magazines and even the championship co-ordinators have been known to get the points wrong, so don't just rely on them for the latest position. Quite often, when low scores are dropped the championship position will be quite different, so make sure you understand the rules, in order that you can advise your driver on his approach to the later rounds.

Plan B

Budgets being what they are, you may not be able to be sure of doing the whole season. Perhaps your funds will at this stage only stretch to the mid-season, at which point you will reassess the situation. It may be that with success, a bit of extra sponsorship or some bonus money, or sheer determination and enthusiasm, you will be able to continue. As well as Plan A you should also have a Plan B; if things don't go as well as expected, you can then cut your losses and go for another objective, or if things go really well and you've already wrapped up the class/category, then you might miss the later rounds and use the funds for a bigger event or rallying abroad. It pays to be flexible and keep the situation under review, but always keep in mind that objective of whatever you do, do it well.

Paperwork

Your paperwork should mostly be straightforward, much as for your earlier events. You should apply for regulations for all the events as soon as possible and chase them up if they don't appear when you feel they should. If there are bonus schemes applicable to your championship, you should apply for these early as sometimes numbers are limited. Concessions on parts and tyres should also be followed up, so that you get the best deal for your driver. The location of the various decals attendant upon such deals should be noted so that the livery of the rally car can be established to give the best visual impact, rather than using a hotch-potch of stickers. Perhaps a nice photo of car and crew, together with sponsor (if any), would be a good idea. You can give this to the local newspaper to use, but it's also useful to send it along with your entry forms for the professional touch, together with a brief press release about the team: driver's and co-driver's biography, details of the car, the programme, and of past results.

Hotels

If the events in your programme are some way from home, you will need to book accommodation. Your budget will determine the quality of this, but Bed & Breakfast houses are obviously

The layout of your sponsorship livery and trade support decals should be carefully co-ordinated to give maximum visual impact, as on this smart Mk 1 Escort. (Lodge.)

good value, so long as the landlady will stand for the odd hours of arriving and departing that rallies sometimes cause. It would be as well to raise this aspect with her before confirming the booking. Quite often, the organizers of bigger events will have a good deal arranged at the Rally HQ hotel, which is well worth choosing so long as you're early enough with your booking. The disadvantage of staying in a Rally HQ is that it can be quite noisy, and if the hotel is not used to rallies, service in the bar and restaurant can be very slow. On the other hand you're close to the organizers, so keeping tabs on official matters and checking results is quite easy. If overseas trips are envisaged, ferry bookings will also have to be made.

It's a good idea to keep a file with copies of all correspondence, in case of later queries. It's good to have some sort of record because if you discover a nice, reasonably priced hotel that's tolerant of rally activities, you might want to use it in later years. On the other hand, if you have a bad experience, make a note of that so that you don't end up there in the future.

Drawbacks

One of the drawbacks to being the co-driver, and therefore the person who organizes things like hotels, is that when it goes wrong in this department, you will get the blame. Regardless of the fact that the hotel the driver or mechanics would have chosen was ten times worse than yours, you must be prepared to be criticized if problems arise. So do your research and make other enquiries if you're at all dubious; if possible, involve your driver/mechanics in the decision-making process—that way they can't blame you entirely if things do go wrong. There is a saying which goes, 'Don't shoot the messenger'. Quite often, because of the nature of co-driving/team organizing, you become that 'messenger'—the bringer of bad news; unfairly, you may be blamed for bad news, even though you're innocent. In time you will develop a broad back, and learn how best to relay your bad news without incurring the wrath of your team-mates.

The team

Getting the rest of the team organized may not be quite so straightforward. Obviously the preparation of the car is basically the driver's responsibility (though I'll come on to the co-driver's 'office' in the next chapter), whether he's doing it 'in house' or through an outside concern. If a major pre-season build/rebuild is under way, the timing of the completion of this is all-important. Try not to turn up on the first event in a just-completed, totally untried car. The chances are it will give trouble. Ideally, the car should be fully complete at least a week before the first round, so that you can have a shake-down. Some crews try to do a small event a couple of weeks before the first proper round, just to iron the 'bugs' out of a new car and for the driver to come to terms with his new or newly-fettled mount. If you can do this, it means you will start your proper assault in confidence and will feel more at home in the car. A good early result can often set you up as 'the team to beat' in the championship, which is a good psychological advantage. Silly errors in the preparation should have been shown up by then and minor improvements effected that should make your first major event more successful.

Service crew

Whereas in the past you may have relied on friends as your service crew, the time has probably come to be a bit more selective. Possibly, the driver has this in hand as part of the preparation deal on the car, but if it is an 'in house' job you need to look at this side of the operation to see if you will get the right sort of back-up crew on your programme. Obviously, it's no good having the best mechanics around if they struggle on the maps and can't actually find the service areas, or if they are accident-prone and don't make the service areas because they're stuck in a ditch. On the other hand, they do have to be good mechanically and know and understand the car, so there's no room for 'hangers-on' either. The service vehicle and trailer also has to be assessed, that the former is properly equipped for the job and that the latter is road-legal and stable with its load. A good service crew will take care of these aspects—it's their 'office' after all—but it doesn't hurt for you to cast a watchful eye over these matters.

Movement schedule

Once you get the final instructions for the first event, you should have enough information to prepare a movement schedule. It doesn't have to be anything elaborate, just brief details of the event, location of start, finish, hotel, ferry details (if any) and other travel arrangements, noise test/trailer parking/scrutineering arrangements, Rally HQ, start number, number of stages, stage mileage, surface details (tarmac, gravel, or mixed). A copy of the final instructions and relevant pages of the regs will suffice. In any case this gives the rest of the team the basic information on the rally, so the service crew knows where it must be and when, and doesn't set off for Kielder when the rest of you are going to South Wales. (Don't laugh, it has happened.) With your (hopefully) extensive knowledge of rallies, such things may seem obvious to you, but others could be less well informed or have their minds on other matters. A simple movement sheet distributed to all the team, as well as to those staying behind (in case they need to make contact urgently), should keep everyone informed and put the team together in the right place at the right time.

Briefcase

Finally, you've probably discovered that the amount of paperwork you need to take on an event has grown to substantial proportions. With all the documents you need for scrutineering and signing on, it's very easy to forget, lose or misplace some vital piece of paper and that's going to impede your progress through documentation. So I tend to carry a 'scrutineering briefcase', in which always live the homologation papers, 'Blue Book' and 'Yellow Book' (the FISA equivalent), championship and event regs, final instructions and a folder with plastic pockets which contain the licences, insurance certificate, registration and membership cards, rally log book and all the other bits of paper you'll have to produce at some time or other. That way you know where everything is kept and it greatly impresses the 'signing on' ladies when you present the

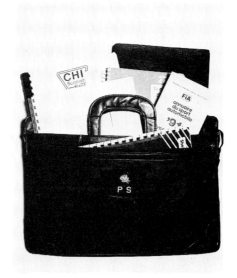

A briefcase is useful to carry all the documents you need for scrutineering and signing on. This is not taken in the car during the event, however.

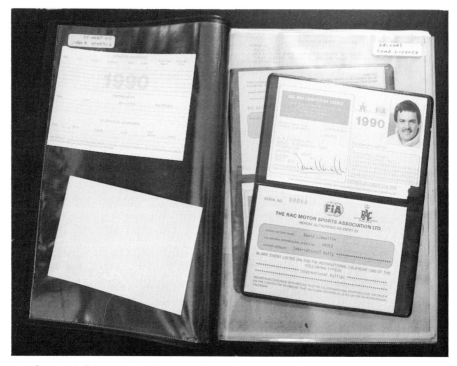

A plastic folder with clear pockets for each document is a good way to keep track of all your paperwork—and to impress the signing-on ladies.

folder, for they can go straight to the item they need and you're not fumbling about in your back pocket looking for the missing bit of paper. Of course, I don't carry this briefcase in the rally car on the event; that would clutter up the 'office', which is part of our next area for close attention.

Chapter 7

Better equipment

Chapters 3 and 5 dealt in some depth with the equipment you will need, so if you have taken my advice fully you should be quite well kitted out by now. Since things are getting a bit more serious, there are a few extras you might like to look at.

We've discussed overalls; well, let's go a stage further and suggest that you also get yourself a set of Nomex underwear

Below left *Nomex underwear is essential in conjunction with Nomex overalls for good protection against fire.* (Lodge.)

Below right *Balaclavas can be of the eye-hole type...* (Lodge.)

Left ...or the open-face type. Seppo Harjanne, 1000 Lakes Rally, 1991. (Kolczak.)

Right A pen/pencil pocket on the sleeve is a good place to keep your writing implements.

to go with them. To be honest, the overalls are nothing like as effective at preventing burns without the underwear, but that underwear will make you feel hotter. This will make you sweat more, especially in a hot rally car under the pressure of competition. If your programme includes Internationals, which last for more than a day, I would advise both you and your driver to get a second set of overalls/underwear, unless neither of you has any sense of smell. For an event like the Lombard RAC Rally, I had a set of overalls and underwear for each of the four days. Incidentally, for some Internationals you will have to produce your overalls at scrutineering; this is so that they can be checked for their homologation mark, so make sure your overalls and other fireproof gear have the FISA approval mark attached.

Ancillary items

To that you should also add set(s) of Nomex socks and, if you wish, balaclavas. I used to think that balaclavas were a bit of a pose, carried over from racing, but in fact when I came to use them I found they absorbed sweat from my head and made my helmet more comfortable, as well as increasing the fire protection. There are two types of balaclava—one with just eye holes and one with a face-sized hole. I would recommend the latter as I feel the eye-hole type can muffle your voice slightly through the material. On the other hand the full-face kind offers better fire protection and can act as a filter on dusty events. If you wear all these items, most of the parts of your body will be covered in fireproof material; unlike the driver, you cannot of course wear fireproof gloves, as you will need the dexterity of your fingers for your various tasks. Hopefully, you will never have to put all this fireproofing to the test.

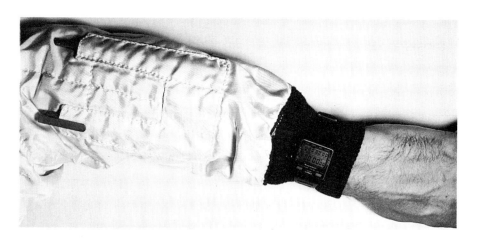

Modifications to overalls

There are some modifications you can make to your overalls. You will need some matching Nomex material and thread (via your supplier or the manufacturer) as well as a willing seamstress. Firstly, I would suggest a pen/pencil pocket on the sleeve; not on the chest, as whatever you put in the pocket can be trapped under the belts and injure you in an accident.

Professional overalls, badged identically for driver and co-driver, make a very good impression. Bernard Occelli and Didier Auriol, Acropolis Rally, 1991. (Lodge.)

Left-hand sleeve if you're right-handed, and vice versa. This gives you easy access to a writing implement whether you're in the car or not, but again doesn't incur the risk of distraction or injury that a 'neck dangler' might provide. If you're doing FISA events outside Britain, the standard continental time card is quite small and can be fitted in a suitably sized pocket/slot on the lower, leg of the overalls. British time cards tend to be bigger and will have to be stowed in the car.

Finally, you will probably need to carry some badges on your overalls for sponsors, trade concerns and manufacturers, as well as your name and blood group. Assuming you and your driver have overalls of the same design, try to arrange a layout of the various badges that is identical on both of you; this gives a more professional appearance. If you're having the overalls made to measure, it should be possible to have your various mods, and even the badging, done by the manufacturer, but this can cost a lot of money.

Rally jacket

I'm afraid I can't recall the last time I actually bought a rally jacket; such items tend to be distributed by sponsors, trade concerns and manufacturers so like me you will perhaps acquire one or more as part of your deal for the season. You can of course buy them through the usual sources. You may find that a winter-weight jacket is much too heavy for summer use and a summer-style too thin for British winters, so either get two types or go for a compromise which will cope with both conditions. If you take your jacket in the rally car, remember that some parts of the rear panels get very hot from the

exhaust system and can melt the fibres of your nice new gear, so proper storage is required.

On the subject of clothing, may I make a plea that you take along with you some alternative clothing for the prizegiving. While you may enjoy the sensation of standing around in the mud-spattered, sweat-encrusted overalls in which you have given your all during the rally, there's no rule that says you must wear them for the prize ceremony. There's always sufficient time from the finish time of the last car to the start of the rizegiving to change out of your working clothes, so there's no excuse for causing offence or distaste as you go up for your reward. Always make the effort to look clean, tidy and presentable on such occasions.

Helmet livery

I also think that a liveried helmet looks professional and provides you with an identity. You may have your own design preference or this may be part of your sponsorship deal. One word of warning: you don't just spray the helmet with any old paint, as some paints can react adversely with the helmet shell, thus destroying its integrity and with it the vital protection of your head. There are specialist helmet painters who will create almost any design you want, but this is an expensive option—you don't have to have it. Don't forget that after the tarting-up process, the helmet must still carry a scrutineer's helmet sticker.

Neck support

Quite a few years ago I had an accident in a rally car which was not fitted with a headrest and consequently I suffered from 'whiplash'. To some extent the problem has remained with me and in time quite a few of us come to suffer from 'Co-driver's Neck'.

Basically, with the weight of your helmet, the act of looking up and down at your map or pace notes, the high 'G' forces (especially on tarmac), as well as unexpected jolts and bumps from the road surface, your neck will suffer quite a lot of strain—more so than the driver's, who will to some extent

Left *Having your helmet liveried looks good, provides an identity and is visible for the in-car TV.* (Lodge.)

Far left *A neck support takes some of the weight of your helmet and can prevent neck injury in the event of a serious accident.*

anticipate the car's movements as a function of his driving and not be moving his head quite so much. While you cannot now go rallying without a headrest, it will still pay you to take care of your neck. After my whiplash, I started to wear a helmet collar or neck support, which is basically a horseshoe-shaped piece of covered, fireproof foam designed to curve around the neck; the helmet sits on the collar and the collar then sits upon your shoulders. These safety items originally came from Formula One at a time when the cars had no suspension movement and the drivers were having trouble keeping their heads still during a race. Initially the collar feels a little restrictive, since it eliminates a lot of the side-to-side movement, but you can still look up and down for note/map reading. Other co-drivers have rejected them because of the movement restriction, but I persevered and found it really helped to take the extra load of the helmet off my neck. There is the added bonus that in the case of a very heavy sideways impact—an impact which can actually break your neck—the collar prevents the head from moving too far. I'm surprised more co-drivers haven't adopted them; you can get them from the specialist shops, but usually only to special order.

Footwear

I don't see the point in co-drivers wearing the same sort of rally boots as drivers. The soles of these are thin to give the driver sensitivity in the use of the pedals. Frankly, I don't think they're ideal for tramping up and down to time controls or pushing a car out of a ditch, as they have very little grip. So my

suggestion would be to get a set of trainers with a good grippy sole and which are reasonably waterproof, but with preferably little or no plastic in the construction (for fire safety reasons). If your driver makes a habit of making you push him out of ditches, perhaps a shoe with a higher side, like a baseball shoe, would help to keep your feet drier in these circumstances. On really muddy events like East African Safari, I have heard of co-drivers wearing rugby boots with studded soles for the extra grip, but for European events these would not be practicable, except perhaps for kicking the errant driver.

Watches

Having already advised you about your rally watch, let me also suggest that you get a second one. Almost all co-drivers have a second watch somewhere: some have them mounted on the dashboard; I prefer the second one on my other wrist. On event, I set one to standard time and leave it in that mode; the other I leave in stop-watch mode, though with rally time already stored in it. This has a double purpose: there's less button-twiddling at crucial times and I have a back-up in case of failure or loss of either watch.

Map magnifier

If you haven't already acquired a map magnifier, now is the time to do so. Not a battery-powered type like you find in motor accessory shops, but a proper 12-volt plug-in type made for the job, with substantial magnifying glass, handle, on/off switch

Far left *Driver boots are not ideal for a co-driver.* (Lodge.)

Left *Some sort of trainer or base-ball shoe with a grippy sole is better, especially when you have to push.*

Right *As well as two different types of trip-meter, Juha Piironen's cockpit has two sets of timepieces —digital (on the dash) and ana-logue (on the door). Safari Rally, 1991.* (Lodge.)

Above left *A map magnifier will become an important part of your equipment for UK rallying.* (Kolczak.)

Above right *A hook or box to store your 'poti' will prevent the lens from becoming scratched when not in use.* (Lodge.)

and rheostat. In days gone by, people used to fabricate their own, but there are several good ones commercially available from specialist motor sporting concerns, so choose the one which has these features and which you find the most comfortable to hold. It'll need a socket somewhere handy in the car, carefully avoiding having the wire passing close to gearlever or handbrake. A hook or storage compartment will prevent it rolling about when not in use. It costs good money—your money—and the lens can be easily scratched, rendering it less

Below left *On road sections you will find headsets almost essential. David Llewellin, 1000 Lakes Rally, 1991.* (Kolczak.)

Below right *Keep them in a storage box to prevent damage.* (Lodge.)

 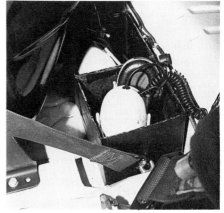

effective, so make sure it gets a proper 'home' in the car. With this device, you can really begin to earn your keep on forestry events.

Headsets

Rally cars are noisy things to live in, even when being driven slowly along on road sections. So that you can communicate with each other on the roads, when not wearing your helmets and so that you don't get a fearful headache from the din, you will each need a pair of headsets. These should be compatible with the intercom system you use for the helmets and so plug into the same sockets. For many people that probably means using the Peltor system, but there are alternatives. You need to have a place to store them where they won't roll about on the floor while you're on the stages. That leads us neatly on to consider 'The Office', your place of work.

'The Office'

If you're going to do a good job as a co-driver, it's clear that you must feel both safe and comfortable. Safety comes from the various aspects we've already covered—roll-cage, seat, belts, fire extinguishers, helmets, overalls, etc.—but all too often insufficient attention is paid to comfort. If you're uncomfortable, you can't do your job properly.

Let's start with the seat. Because I am a tall person, I've always had to spend quite a bit of time sorting out my seat position, much to the chagrin of the various rally mechanics who have had to attend to the modifications I've needed. But whatever your stature, the ideal seat position should be 'low down and far back'. Generally speaking, this is the best situation for the rally car, for the lower your weight, the lower the centre of gravity of the car in stage trim, which is better for the handling. The further back you are, the better the balance of the car, for usually the greater mass (of engine, gearbox, etc.) is towards the front and when the rear wheels are driven, more weight to the rear improves traction.

However, if you're small or the car has a high dashboard line, you could end up being too low and so not actually be able to see outside. Some people might suggest it's better if you can't see outside, for that way you won't get frightened, but in practice you are going to have to relate to the outside world when you come to read maps or pace notes. Usually, seat-mounting brackets for competition seats have holes for adjustable heights, so it's really a question of trial and error

Left *Low down and far back is the ideal location for the co-driver's seat.* (Kolczak.)

Below *Getting both seat and foot plate into the correct position takes some sorting out. Here Luis Moya checks out his fitting in a new rally car.* (Lodge.)

until you get it right for you. In my case, quite often the seat brackets had to be dispensed with to get me low enough when helmeted to clear the roof; in this case, the seat can be bolted directly to the floor.

With the much more substantial roll-cages in use these days, it may become harder to move your seat back as far as you would like, otherwise some part of the seat will foul on the cage. It is actually a drawback to have the roll-cage too close to your seat, because during the course of a stage your seat will flex and make contact; this will certainly distract you from your tasks. There is a FISA rule now on homologated cars which prohibits the back of your (or the driver's) seat being

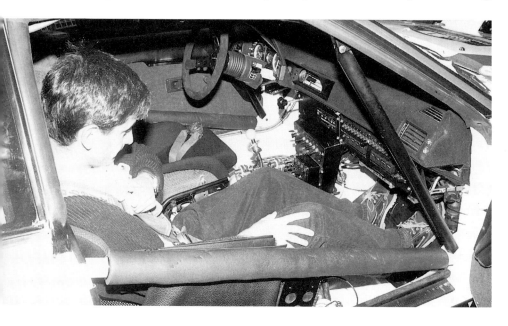

further back than the front edge of the original rear seat when fitted. So do check on a standard production model for this dimension before finalizing your seat position.

Rake

The next thing to get right is the seat rake. I find it's no good sitting bolt upright: it's very uncomfortable and soon gives me a numb posterior. So you need a bit of rake—not too much—to get a good working position. This is done by putting packing washers on the front seat bolts (if vertically attached) or by raising the front bolt holes only, if it's a horizontal attachment. Again it's a case of trial and error and you may well find that getting the right rake affects the position of the seat upon the floor or in relation to the roll-cage. You can see why it must infuriate rally mechanics, who clearly have better things to do than to fiddle about all day with the co-driver's seat. But it's worth getting it right, in the end.

Footplate

Once you've got the seat more or less right, you can establish some other things—the position of the foot plate, for instance. If you couldn't get the seat back as far as you would have liked, then the foot plate may have to go forward. You should end up with a position in which your legs are neither straight out, nor bent or splayed excessively, just slightly bent and remaining so even when you apply firm pressure to the foot plate. The rake of the foot plate can be wrong too, which will give you an uncomfortable foot position, so check that out also. When you've finally got all these positions correct, they should give you a comfortable position and a firmly based lap, which is in effect your office desk-top.

Belts

Your next task is to get the belt positions correct in relation to the seat. The original fittings may or may not be in the right place, but check that the belts are not kinked as they pass through to the seat, nor rubbing against some sharp object. Both of these faults will impair the belts' ability to hold you in the event of an accident. If you have the crutch-strap type, fit a piece of padding around the crutch-strap hole in the seat; this is to stop the belts falling through the hole when not in use, as they're very difficult to recover once they've dropped down.

The mounting of the seat belts and their clear routing through the seat holes is important for safety and effectiveness. (Kolczak.)

Padding

I've mentioned padding on the roll-cage; this is still important. When strapped in, try to move your head, arms and legs about and see what they come into contact with; if it's sharp, the offending item must be repositioned; if it's hard, pad it. In my days in the Audi Quattros, I had a specially padded cover for the handbrake mechanism, which otherwise would connect with pinpoint accuracy on my 'funny bone'. This item became known as my 'model railway tunnel' because of its shape, but it was very effective.

Helmet storage

Once you're strapped in, try getting at your crash helmets in their storage place. In today's increasingly restricted cockpits, with ever more convoluted roll-cages, access to the rear of the cockpit may be seriously compromised. Sometimes you need the arms of a gorilla to extract the helmets from the rear, so do give this aspect some thought, as it's likely to be you who has to pass the helmets over. In the Toyota Celica, which had a very small cockpit, David Llewellin's helmet was stored in the front footwell under my legs, with my helmet alone in the back. There are several solutions, you just have to work on them.

Storage

Provision for storage is the next problem. You will need somewhere to stow time cards, road book, maps, pace notes and all your other in-car paraphernalia. Not necessarily all in the same place. The time card is vital: without it, you're out of the rally, so this needs a safe location, dedicated to this item

Above left *Good in-car storage is essential if you are not to lose vital documents in the event of an inversion. Dougie Paterson gropes for his paperwork after Andrew Wood's roll on the '90 Manx. (Kolczak.)*

Above right *This large zippable mail sack is a good idea, though the map light position is not the best. (Lodge.)*

Below *Elasticated pockets are good for time cards. (Kolczak.)*

Bottom *This Lancia has several storage pockets, all with Velcro flaps and clear of the floor. (Lodge.)*

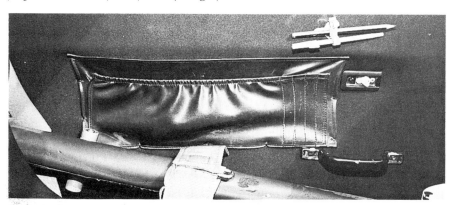

only. Quite simply, if the time card shares its location with, for example, the road book, it's all too easy for the time card to be spilled out when the road book is extracted. In Europe, time cards tend to be smaller but in the UK they seem to be around A4 size or slightly narrower. I would recommend an elasticated or, better still, zipped pocket (to retain the time card in the event of an inversion) somewhere on the door. That way, you can get at it easily and it's in a place which shouldn't get wet. Things on or near the floor do get wet, so whatever storage you arrange for your maps, road book and other susceptible items should be waterproof and clear of the floor. Most co-drivers take with them a rally bag for carrying pace notes, regulations, bulletins and other oddments. This too should be waterproof; a set of sodden pace notes, rendered almost unreadable, is hardly going to impress your driver, even if it's his poor preparation of the car that has brought about the influx of water.

I tend to have several separate stowage places: map pocket on the door; road book/pace note book sized pocket by my left leg (in a RHD car); map box behind the driver's seat; rally bag (containing less vital items) behind my seat; small pouch for pencils, Romer, rubber, map light bulbs, etc. attached to the door; pencil clip on the door panel; torch in a tube on the roll-cage; map magnifier stowage in front of my seat; headset stowage on rear roll-cage; jacket in netting stowage in rear side panels. Unfortunately, all these items add weight to the car, so they should be made of lightweight, fireproof materials and be as small as possible. Obviously, if you overdo things and clutter up the car with too much of your stuff, you are unlikely to endear yourself to a team which has embarked on a major weight-saving exercise on the car. On the other hand, you have to be able to do your job properly, so sometimes it's a question of compromise between the two sides. You can always drop into the discussion that an unhappy co-driver can be hell on the mechanics, in which case they may grant all your requests. On the other hand they may go to the driver and suggest that an easier solution would be a different, less demanding co-driver.

Radio

These days many rally cars have a two-way radio or CB unit fitted. If this is the case for your car, I suggest you have it mounted where the switches and knobs are accessible for the co-driver, because it's you who will operate it most of the time. In fact, you don't just switch it on at the start of the event and

Two-way radios are quite common now and a useful tool if used correctly. The microphone should be mounted in a position handy for driver and co-driver. (Lodge.)

forget about it, as it's likely to burst into life mid-stage (as the service crew perhaps discuss how they've managed to get lost—again) and distract you. So you need to be able to turn it on and off easily. Some cars have a single switch somewhere, just for this purpose, but some radios need lots of button-pressing and bezel-twiddling to get them in the correct mode, which is bad news for a co-driver. See if you can simplify this arrangement, as its complication will impinge upon your work-load. However, the microphone should be in a position which can be reached by both you and the driver, as there will be times when the driver will need to discuss a particular techni-cal problem with your service crew; you may be busy with your own work, particularly at a stage finish (which is where most car problems are reported) or you may not wish to act as a go-between when a heated discussion is taking place. In both cases, it's better if the driver can speak directly, so have the microphone placed where he can get at it. I'll discuss radio techniques in a later chapter.

Technical items

You might think that technical items are not your province at all. Let me tell you a little story. On the 1989 Ulster Rally, David Llewellin and I were driving a brand-new Toyota which had several things different from the old car. One of these was a fuse for the engine management system. The car was so new and so recently finished that, apart from scrutineering, I'd barely sat in it. Consequently, when the 'brain' (the car's, not mine) popped its fuse mid-stage and the car stopped, neither of us knew what to look for and we lost several crucial minutes looking in all the wrong areas before we found the popped-out fuse. If I'd known more about that car's intricacies, a loss of several minutes would have been just a few seconds and we might well have won the event, instead of coming third. The moral? Know your rally car.

This applies to several areas. You should know and understand the gauges, because the driver might not always spot a temperature gauge which is reading way over normal, with expensive results. The fuel gauge may be on your side anyway; in theory, if somebody's done their sums right, you shouldn't be running out of fuel, but it does happen, so get used to monitoring it and understanding its eccentricities—they are not the most reliable items anyway. Get to know what the various switches do; you may be required to activate some of them (e.g wipers, washers) when the driver's hands are full of opposite lock. You need to be able to go to them instantly in this situation, even in the dark.

We covered fuses, but if they're the replaceable, rather than the pop-out, type, know where the spares are positioned, for rapid replacement. You also need to know about the switches for the extra lights; you may need to operate these at scrutineering or while the driver is adjusting them outside the car. If there are spares for the engine management system or other

Below left *Get to know the complexities of your rally car, from the humble club car...* (Hodson/CCC.)

Below right *...to a full works-spec car.* (Kolczak.)

Jack and wheelbrace should be securely stored, but also readily accessible as sometimes you need to be able to get to them in a hurry. (Kolczak.)

such items that might give trouble mid-stage, make sure you know what to do to swop over; quite often these items are mounted at your side of the car. The point I'm making is, don't be afraid to ask what might seem quite simple questions, so that you really understand the workings of the car. That way you can contribute more in times of difficulty. Get to know what the car feels like when it's working normally, so that when something looks, sounds or even smells odd, you notice it.

Jack and wheelbrace

I'll deal with the job of wheel changing in the 'Problems' chapter later, so for now all you need to do is establish the storage positions of the jack and wheelbrace. There are several solutions to this problem, but whatever is decided do make sure these items are securely located. They're hard, heavy and uncomfortable things and a rap on the body from a loose jack during a stage is not a pleasant occurrence, believe me. The same applies to a spare wheel, which if not properly secured can cause very serious injury if it comes forward, say, in the course of an accident. So make sure you know where these articles are secured and how to extract them and replace them. A small tool roll should be present in the car, with not too many items, just the essential ones; again this should be readily accessible but securely stowed.

Intercoms

In all probability you already have one intercom system. I think it would be wise to have a back-up, plumbed in alongside the main system. Like all things, the intercom can pack up, so it's a good idea to have a spare that you can swop over to straight away, even mid-stage. If your main system is driven by the car's electrical system, it would make sense for your back-up to be powered by its own battery; that way, if the problem lies in the electrical system, it doesn't affect the spare intercom. Once again, tape the sockets to the upper belts, paired left-hand to left-hand and right to right, so you can go to them immediately, even in the dark.

Some teams have the radio connected to the intercom, so that you can hear via the headsets; this is acceptable, so long as it in no way compromises the operation of the intercom, though in my experience it can lead to interference or even failure, or complication with extra cables and so on. Both are undesirable, so if you choose this method, make sure it's right.

The list

I think it's highly unlikely that you will get all of the foregoing items sorted at one go before the season has begun. This will depend on the available time and, of course, money. If you can't get everything done, just go for the items which you consider most important and keep a list of what is outstanding. Space prohibits me from mentioning every single item you might need to sort out for your 'office', so no doubt you will come upon some particular 'tweak' for your particular car and for your particular requirements which is not mentioned here. If so, just add it to the list, and keep that list under review. Invariably, you will find some things amiss on your first event with the car.

A seat position not quite right when you use it on stages, a storage pocket which takes in water, some place where you always bang your leg, an unwanted reflection on the windscreen. I always used to write these jobs down on the back page of my road book, otherwise I would tend to forget them when away from the environment of the rally car. Then, soon after the event, I would rewrite the list, together with the left-over items, and give it to the mechanics for attention. Soon it would become a matter of pride to get that list shorter or even eliminate it altogether for future events, by which time your 'office' should have become exactly how you wanted it. Persistence is a virtue.

Chapter 8

Better co-driving

No matter how well equipped your rally car, if you yourself aren't up to scratch as a co-driver, you're soon going to be found out. Perhaps now is the time to do a little soul-searching, a little self-analysis, to see if you're really cut out for this job. Not everyone is, of course. You may have found, for instance, that car sickness is a problem you cannot solve. Perhaps business or family pressures are going to prevent you from competing. You might be utterly honest with yourself and say that fear has had its effect, particularly if you've had some bad early experiences. Even the very nature of the job is anathema to some people—all that navigating, timekeeping and calculation, not to mention the sometimes none-too-comfortable interior of a rally car or the pressure of competition, all for little or no reward or recognition—there have got to be better ways of spending one's leisure days. For some people.

If, however, the rallying you have done so far has filled you with enthusiasm and the urge to do much more, and you are in a position to do so, then read on. Even if you feel your lack of experience is against you, or that you are error-prone, if you have the will to persevere, you will in time overcome these problems. But to achieve that you will have to become a committed co-driver; no half-measures; from now on things get a bit more serious—enjoyable, but serious too.

Mistakes

In rallying there is no substitute for experience. This applies to drivers, mechanics, engineers and team managers and is particularly true in the case of co-drivers. So by taking part in more rallies, you will be confronted by an increasing number of situations which will test you mentally and physically. You will find that some situations you coped with rather well (though don't expect your driver to have spotted them—he'll just take things for granted); there will be some situations which slightly caught you out or which you could have handled better, but you managed to fumble your way through in the end (he probably didn't notice); and there will be things which you definitely got wrong (for sure, he won't have missed those).

Take every opportunity to learn from your mistakes—and those of other co-drivers: analyse the mistakes, work out why they happened and plan to avoid them in the future. By recognizing a situation which can create an error, you can be one jump ahead of the opposition the next time it crops up. It's a strange situation: drivers can make loads of mistakes, go off the road, hit rocks, break the gearbox by sheer brutality, or whatever, and it's just accepted as the norm—part of the pressure of competition. If a co-driver makes an understandably human error in similar circumstances, he's generally jumped on from a great height and pilloried by all and sundry. It's all very unfair.

We all make mistakes; I've made them, every top co-driver has made them, you too will make them. Sometimes they can be avoided in the pre-event planning stage of the rally. Once you receive the regulations and final instructions, you should read them really carefully, even if they look like every other set of regs you've received, just to see if there's anything tricky in them. Make sure you understand what the organizers mean; sometimes they don't mean what they say, or don't say what they mean, but in case of ambiguity, check with another competitor, or with the organizers themselves so that you can understand what their intentions are.

The same advice applies to the road book or route when you receive it. Don't just plot it on the maps and forget about it—really take that route apart and analyse: Are the road sections timed correctly (50 mph max on motorways, 30 mph on other roads)? Do they run through big towns where traffic might be heavy? If so, are there alternatives that you might take in case of a blockage? If there are alternative service areas, which are the most favourable positions? How much service time is there? How much fuel will you need at the service points? When will you need the spotlights fitting? Are some stages cleanable (check last year's times if stages are similar)? What are the maximum times (if any) on the stages? Is there a stage with a significantly different surface for which you will need different tyres? The list goes on and on. All these questions will require answers in order for you to complete the service schedule, which we'll look at in the next chapter.

Let me tell you a cautionary tale about the Welsh Rally one year, which included repeated stages on the Epynt military ranges. One particular stage had an identical start and finish point for the first and the second time of visiting. A top co-driver assumed that the stage route was also identical on both visits. It wasn't—with the effect that the crew took the wrong route on the second occasion and were excluded. The worse thing you can say as a co-driver is 'I assumed'. You should assume nothing. Check it out beforehand.

Without being too much of a pessimist, I like to pose the question 'What if...?' and then think of the things which can possibly go wrong in a particular section of the route, and what I can plan or arrange in advance to mitigate the problem. Of course, I can't foresee every eventuality, but the more common occurrences, such as a puncture or a long delay at the stage start, can be interjected at the planning stage. If you think about these possibilities and their consequences, you're less likely to get caught out when they do happen, in which case you're less likely to compound the problem with a pressure-induced error on your part. Forethought is half the battle.

Once the event is under way, you'll just have to keep your wits about you. Use your eyes and ears—even your nose—for they can tell you of potential difficulties ahead. Keep an eye on the weather in the direction of the rally route; if it seems to be changing, that could herald a different tyre choice. If the stages are dusty, are you able to hang back an extra minute or two, to give your driver clearer air? If there's snow about, is it freezing?—in which case you should get into the stage right on time before it polishes. Or is it thawing?—in which case you should go in later and let others clear the track for you. (This of course depends on whether you would incur road penalties for being late.) Are other co-drivers talking about some route or timing anomaly that has caught them out? Is there some place in a forthcoming stage which they speak of in awe, since it has tricked lots of others? Listening out for such gems can save you from similar ignominy.

Clearly, I can't list every possible situation which might cause you difficulty, but by being aware, you can hopefully avoid some of the pitfalls. The most likely times for you to make an error are (a) when you're under pressure, perhaps at the end of a stage or on a short road section when you've got lots of things to do and very little time to carry them out, and (b) when you're relaxed, on a long road section or on your way to the finish. If you're under pressure, my advice is to force yourself to keep calm and look at things carefully and logically.

 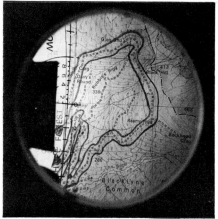

Above left *Check, check, check. Howard Davies double-checks his time cards before leaving a stage finish—a likely place to make a mistake. 1000 Lakes Rally, 1990. (Kolczak.)*

Above right *A special stage as seen on a 1:50,000 series map through a map magnifier. (Lodge.) (© Crown copyright.)*

Stick to your established routines and don't get flustered. Ask, nay tell, the driver to keep quiet while you do your job and work things out. If you can keep your head while others are losing theirs...so the saying goes. On relaxed sections, the watchword is 'concentrate'; that's an integral part of co-driving anyway, but do be on guard for the unforced error.

On the maps

Reading the maps to assist the driver is a skill which is almost entirely unique to the British co-driver. Because many of us cut our teeth on the highly popular road events of the 1960s, 1970s and early 1980s, it was only to be expected that we would try to carry that skill over to special stage rallying. Many people were sceptical at first of the benefits and I must admit it took me a while to develop the skill so that it actually became a help to the driver and not a hindrance. Reading off the map will only assist the driver if the information is reliable; in some places the 1:50,000 maps were far from that. So if you tried to read the road in this situation, you were giving the driver false information, which would either slow him down too much, or cause him to go off the road.

If you persevered, you could develop a 'feel' for the forest as portrayed on the map. If you knew the map didn't work in a particular forest, you told the driver so and let him drive unaided. The accuracy situation was much improved when the 1:25,000 maps came into use, though it was some time before the RAC MSA 'legalized' them on safety grounds. This series of maps was undergoing a thorough revision (the first series was not much use for rally purposes, being seriously out of date) and the new versions laid most of the forests' secrets bare. Just take a section of forestry on a 1:50,000 and compare it with the same forest on a 1:25,000 and you'll see what I mean.

Of course, you don't have to use the map; many co-drivers survive on road book alone. The road book should, I repeat, should, give you sufficient information to negotiate the stage safely. Alas, this is not always the case. While you shouldn't get lost with the road book, trip-meter, arrows and caution boards, you may well not get the full story. Perhaps on your early forest rallies, you might feel that using the map is too big a step. That's fair enough for a beginner, but you really should be looking to make use of the map at the earliest opportunity, if only not to waste the valuable opportunity being presented. Discuss the situation with your driver and see how he feels about it. He must understand that even as he is on a learning curve with the driving, so are you with the co-driving and map-reading. If you are working off the map for the first time, he must make allowances as you work your way into the system. When I first started reading off the map, my driver was John Taylor, a hard task-master, but he encouraged me, even when I got it wrong, knowing that it would come right in the end and he would ultimately benefit.

The sooner you can get into reading off the map the better, because firstly you will get more satisfaction from the contribution you are making and secondly, you will learn your way around the forests much, much sooner. Off the road book, one forest is very much like another; off the map, they come alive and imprint themselves on your memory. One word of warning though: don't try to use road book and map simultaneously—it doesn't work. The difference in nature of the two media means that you can only keep your place on one of them.

Marking the maps

The regulations for your forest rallies will specify the 1:50,000 maps you require. They usually specify the 1:25,000 as well, but in case they don't you can get a key plan from the Ordnance Survey which will show you the 1:25,000 maps you need to cover the forests of the event. Obviously you don't need to get them for the whole rally route, just the stages. There are rally map suppliers who will, for a fee, provide prefabricated maps with a laminate covering for all the regular forests. The advantage of the laminate covering is that you can clean off an old route and use the map again on subsequent events. I preferred to make my own, partly because of possible OS revisions and partly because I tended to keep the old routes as a record. Each rally done added to the file of information, which could be referred to prior to subsequent visits to the same forests. It took a bit of time before each event to make up the maps, but I was usually happy with the result. Often I had to cut up two or three maps to get the complete forest, but I then mounted them on A4-sized pieces of thin cardboard, which was usually big enough for all but the very big forest stages. (In this case I cut the map at a convenient point and mounted the rest on the reverse of the card.) This then provided me with a firm base and a convenient, manageable size of map to read. Some organizers reproduce the map with the stage marked on it in the road book, but usually the detail deteriorates in the copying/printing process, so this type of map is not as good to use as the original item.

As and when you are given the stage routes, you can then mark these onto the maps. I experimented with several colours before I settled on a thin orange felt-tip pen, which provided a good contrast with the green of the forest without obscuring

Below left *Laminate-covered 1:25,000 series are popular for the UK forests. (Lodge.)*

Below right *Or you can make up your own, mounted on card. (© Crown copyright.)*

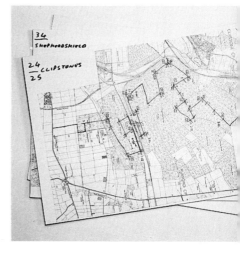

detail, but it's all a matter of preference. The Blue Book states that you can put on the map any information provided by the organizers, plus any official 'Black Spots' (ie RAC MSA-nominated hazard points). So, using an ultra-fine waterproof black pen I then marked on all the cautions, notations, junction shapes (if tricky-looking or not-as-map), junction numbers and junction distances. Why the last two? Well, being generally benevolent souls, the stage start marshals will usually tell you about something dodgy—a pile of logs, some deep mud or another competitor 'off' somewhere in the forest. Their description of the place will usually be 'half a mile after junction 7' or 'about 3½ miles in'. If you've got to riffle through your road book to pinpoint where that is, you may struggle to locate it on the map before the stage countdown. But with junction numbers and distances already on the map, you can go straight to it. Why a waterproof pen? Well, just try a non-permanent ink and see what happens to your beautiful maps when it rains or your palms get a bit sweaty. The resultant mess soon makes your precious maps illegible.

Precious maps they are, too. Apart from the cost and time of making them up, you will accumulate knowledge from them that will stand you in good stead later on. However, let me warn you now that you are not allowed to mark information on these maps which is not provided by the organizers. If your motor club expert tells you about a bend where everyone went off last year, don't mark it on your map. You just have to remember it or keep it on a 'master' map which you don't use

In situations like these, rally cars are not always fully waterproof, so keep your maps and pace notes well clear of the floor. (Lodge.)

on the rally. It helps if you try to visualize from the map the characteristics of the road leading up to such places.

A lot of people suspected that I had pace notes written on my maps, but I can honestly say they were quite 'clean'. I would store useful information on old maps after a rally and then refer to those maps before the next event to use those particular forests, but I never, ever, took them in the rally car. That way you build up your own file of information and make yourself develop a good memory for the forests. Of course, it does mean you have to make up new maps for each rally— more time and expense, I'm afraid' but it's worth it, as in time you will build up a veritable library of stage information.

As you come to do bigger events, especially Internationals, you will need to take more maps with you in the car. Rather than carry the whole lot around with you, separate them into 'legs' (perhaps with a different coloured sticker on the cover) and take only the essential ones with you. Leave the rest in the 'chase car' or whatever—but don't forget to collect them before the start of the next leg. That way you'll not weigh down the rally car unnecessarily.

Finally, rally cars are not known for being the most water-proof of vehicles, so always keep your maps, for road and stage, in a leak-proof bag or plastic holder when in the car and only take them out as and when you need them.

Reading the map

You need to come to some agreement with the driver as to how you're going to 'call' the information out from the map. Try to stick to fairly simple descriptions. 'Fast', 'Medium', 'Ninety' (degrees) and 'Hairpin' is one way and will certainly do for starters. Use 'Caution' and 'Danger' sparingly. It will take you a bit of time to get the distances right, especially if you've got used to 1:50,000 maps. What you have here is an embryonic pace note system (of which more later) and in the light of experience you may both find that you're not entirely happy with it. But these are early days and it's quite possible to tinker with your method, develop and refine it as you go along. The important thing is that you've made a start; next time, it will be better.

After putting the route on the map, if you've got time, try running through each stage mentally and verbally, saying to yourself how you will describe each straight, each corner, each hazard, each incline. It's good practice and that way a tricky sequence becomes less of a panic when you arrive there for real, so you can call it coolly, clearly and concisely. No doubt, if

Right *The co-driver checks road book and map and mentally runs through the features of the stage before the start.* (Lodge.)

Below *The map will not tell you about a pile of gravel on the inside of a corner.* (Lodge.)

someone catches you doing this and muttering away to yourself in a corner, it will only convince them of what they already suspected—that all co-drivers are mentally unhinged.

David Llewellin uses a number system for his pace notes, so for a while we also tried to use numbers in the forests. In the end, because of the precision of his number system, we came to the conclusion that it didn't really work for the more flexible nature of reading off the map, so we reverted to words for 'blind' forestry, though still retaining numbers for true pace notes. This underlines that there is still a different style of driving when the information comes from the map. The reason is that the map cannot tell you everything; it doesn't tell you about a pile of logs, a tree stump on the inside, a ditch on the outside, a sudden change of surface from dry to mud or a particularly rough section. So the driver has to drive with some margin to allow for the unexpected.

The skill of map-reading has often been called the 'Black Art' of rallying, for there is an indefinable element of 'feel', which not all co-drivers can achieve. Once you do get it right, there's tremendous satisfaction because it works so well, it's almost as good as pace notes. Although I am a Yorkshireman, I never rallied in the Yorkshire forests any more than my co-driving peers, yet I developed a rapport, a 'feel' for those forests that brought for my drivers a psychological and a real advantage whenever we were there. I sincerely hope that the present trend towards pace-noting our forests does not eventually eliminate this wonderful skill that we have here in Britain, for that would eliminate the enjoyment and challenge of 'blind' forestry rallying.

Road book preparation

After your maps, the next item which should receive your specialist attention is the road book, because this effectively becomes your 'bible' during the rally. It will already tell you most of what you know, but you can make quite a few improvements. This will take a bit of time and effort, but is well worth it, especially when the chips are down, on the rally itself.

Starting from the front, first of all put your name on it. That way, hopefully it'll find its way back to you if you're careless enough to lose it and you won't get it mixed up with someone else's. Next, go through the road book with a highlighter pen and mark up all the time controls, passage controls and so on. This is so that you don't actually miss them; don't laugh—I've known even professional co-drivers miss a passage control

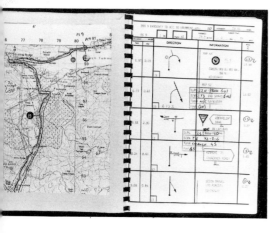

The road book requires quite a lot of preparation to give you all the information at your fingertips. (© Crown copyright.)

situated in a lay-by, because they weren't really expecting it. While you've got a highlighter in your hand, mark the important instructions, like which time cards you should hand in at which point, and if there are any serious warnings about speed from the organizers or the possibility of police radar.

Then you should add the service points—their location in the road book, the service point number (if taken from a proper service schedule), the service vehicle(s) there, how much service time you should have if the road section has gone to plan, how much fuel you should have in the fuel tank as you leave the service point, what tyres you should put on, and any other anticipated jobs (fit lights, etc). I had a rubber stamp made with boxes for each of these, to keep the road book tidy.

At the top of each page I put the amount of 'slack' in the road section, which is the same as service time normally, but even on pages where there was no service point. That way, if we ran into problems—roadworks, spectator traffic, technical difficulties—I knew how much time I had to play with before we got behind time. You have to take each road section on its merits to calculate this. On normal roads, you should have no problem averaging 40 mph, if—and it's a big 'if'—there are no hold-ups, no sections through busy towns, no parts near a spectator access point where there could be queues, and so on. On big main roads, you can usually manage a 50 mph average; on narrow country lanes, not much over 30 mph. Try to be realistic in these calculations.

On the same basis, I also add in the right-hand column my 'countdown' figure, that is, how long it's going to take me from certain junctions to reach the next time control. That way, I can control the pace of the road section; if we've spent a bit too long in service, I can see instantly how big the problem is and ask for a speed increase. By monitoring it at each junction, I can see if the situation is getting better and then relax the pace a little.

Here are a few more hints: if the stage is the same as last year's, I put down relevant times ready for comparison with this year's. Sometimes the stage minimum time and maximum time (if any) are going to be important to you, so write them down at the stage exit box, as usually the organizers don't put them there, which is where you might need to know them. The time of stage opening is also of interest, especially if you're running near the head of the field, so write that down near the stage start. Sometimes, I put a photocopy of the stage map and its environs on a blank page of the road book (if not already provided by the organizers), so that I can find my way to the service in an emergency, without fumbling for a map in a hurry.

Top left *This is the correct sequence of boards for a time control: yellow advance board...* (Lodge.)

Top right *...red board at the control point...* (Lodge.)

Above left *...beige end of control zone board.* (Lodge.)

Above right *If a stage start is involved, the first two boards are followed by a red stage start board.* (Lodge.)

If pace notes are involved, write down the book and page number, so you can go straight to the correct set of notes . You should end up with a road book which is absolutely stuffed with all sorts of information. Without doing the work I've described, you might have to dig out other documents, or riffle through the front of the road book to find what you need. But this way, it's all there in front of you and when the pressure's really on, you can come up with the right answers, as well as take a bit of heat off yourself. By being cool and in full control, you will do a good job and make a favourable impression all round.

Control boards

Whereas on your Club and Restricted rallies, time controls were probably fairly relaxed matters, you will find as you move up in event status that these points are rather more formal. Firstly, do you really know the correct sequence of control boards as laid down by FISA? They are as follows:
    Yellow Board (with clock symbol)—start of time control area.
    Red Board (with clock symbol)—position of time control.
    Beige Board (with slanting bars)—end of time control area.
    If the control is also at the start of a stage, the beige board comes after the:
    Red Board (with flag)—stage start position.
    Remember that Parc Fermé rules apply within all controls, including the stage start and stage finish zones—you can-not work on the car even if it goes wrong on the start or stop line. You must still push it clear of the beige board.
    Finally, for the stage finish there's the:
    Yellow Board (with chequered flag)—warning of the stage finish coming up.
    Red Board (with chequered flag)—flying finish position.
    Motorway-type countdown boards (three bars, two bars, one bar)—slowing-down zone.
    Red 'Stop' board—stop line.
    There can be minor local variations to this system and of course you may encounter several other official boards mid-stage to indicate various hazards, as well as the arrowing system we dealt with earlier. Some events will also erect boards to indicate the position of a mid-stage radio or safety/rescue point. In all, the organizers have to erect quite a lot of boards in the correct setting-out of a stage.
    If the finish incorporates a time or passage control, you should still get the same relevant boards, followed by the beige (end of control area) board.
    A passage control has the same sequence of coloured

This page *At the finish you will get a yellow advance board followed by a red flying finish board at the timing point. Motorway-style countdown boards then lead you to the red stop board, at which your time will be entered on your time card. Once again, this is followed by an end of control board.* (Lodge.)

Opposite above *During the stage you may encounter several hazard signs, like these for (left to right) bad bend, bad double bend and narrow bridge.* (Lodge.)

boards as a basic time control, but with a 'stamp' symbol instead of a clock.

Just as important, make sure your driver understands the meaning of the various boards. When I first started rallying with David Llewellin, I was surprised that he didn't really know about the various boards for time controls, passage controls and so on; he would slow down at the yellow board before a stage flying finish, or stop outside a passage control yellow board, or even want to work on the car in a control. But, on

reflection, he'd just come out of British National Championship rallying, which used to be rather lax in respect of control signalization and policing, so perhaps it wasn't so surprising after all.

The significance of the yellow time control board is that your car should only pass it when you are within one minute before your due time. If you go in earlier than that, the marshal is quite within his rights to book you in on the next minute, with attendant time penalty. Quite often, earliness penalties are double, treble, or even worse, than lateness penalties, so clearly they are to be avoided at all costs. Once your car is at the control, you should present the time card only when the minute you want has arrived. Again the marshal is empowered to give you the time at which you present the card, so if you give it to him early, you will suffer the consequences. Remember, you are not allowed to work on the car within a control zone, so wait until the car is beyond the beige board before carrying out any emergency repairs. The exception to this is that you may clean the windscreen or lights. You may also change a puncture, using wheel and equipment carried in the car, for which there is usually an allowance of five or six minutes, which should be plenty. However, the marshal must

Right *This is the sign for a passage control, at which time cards are collected for results processing.* (Lodge.)

agree to this work and sign your time card to signify this. Normally, however, you have just three minutes from check in at the time control to starting the stage; if due to your own fault you take more than this, you can be penalized for failing to start the stage at the specified time. Of course, if you just scraped into the time control on the 59th second of your minute, you will have somewhat less than two minutes to the start of the stage by the time the formalities are completed.

Timing systems

Just to confuse you, there are actually two types of timing system in Britain: there is the standard FISA system which times from stage start to next time control, and there is the Target Time system which times from stage finish to next time control. In my view there is no question that the Target Time system is better in several respects, but the dictates of our sporting masters in Paris mean that its acceptance is limited to our lesser events. Not all co-drivers share my view—it's a matter of personal preference.

Once you understand the differences, the actual timekeeping side is quite similar. The operation of the controls is the same; the stages are timed in the same way. The Target Time system will incorporate a minimum time for the stage, so if you beat this time you will still receive the minimum time (ie the stage was 'cleaned'). There will also be a maximum time for the stage, beyond which you will incur road penalties as well as the time loss on the stage. Remember to keep a note of these, otherwise you could be closer to exclusion than you think. The FISA system doesn't incorporate a maximum time (and usually not a minimum time either), but you may suffer lateness penalties at the next time control if delayed mid-stage, as time thus lost comes out of your road section time. On Target Time, this doesn't happen. So make sure you know which system you're working to, otherwise you'll end up in a mess with the timekeeping. Also, note that the running order tends to change more on Target Time, since faster cars gradually move up the order and slower cars, or those with problems, move down. One advantage of this is that if there have been errors in the seeding of an event, Target Timing tends to adjust these naturally. On the FISA system you can end up stuck behind the same slow car for stage after stage. With Target Timing, so long as the marshals adhere to their 'stage open' time, each stage start works as a mini regroup, keeping the rally closed up, which makes for better safety and event management.

If you have been delayed and are late at a control, you will

Above *Here's a nice tidy queue waiting outside a time control, leaving room for late-comers to drive up the outside. It isn't always as orderly as this.* (Lodge.)

Right *The co-driver of the Peugeot holds his driver outside the yellow time control board, waiting for his minute to come up, while the two previous cars carry out the checking in process within the control. Good time control technique is important.* (Lodge.)

first have to work your way round a queue of later runners outside the time control, not all of whom will be expecting your hurried arrival. Get your card to the marshal as quickly as you can (sometimes you may have to run up to him, if your car is blocked in the queue). If he's a kind soul, or a bit flustered, he might just give you the time you ask for, though your fellow co-drivers might raise their eyebrows at this. However, if indeed you are given a later time, you will have to run in a later position in rally order—you can't normally jump the queue back to your original slot.

So, having brushed up on your own contribution to the team effort and the management of your own operations, let us now look at the management of the service crew and see if we can improve their contribution to the team effort.

137

Chapter 9

Service matters

Whatever the size of your rally team, you will need to develop a good relationship with your service crew. This applies whether you're a small team, relying on friends and club mates for service, or a more professional outfit with a bigger complement of personnel. While the efforts of the service crew might seem primarily directed towards the car and the driver, these people will simply be unable to function properly on events without a fair amount of input from yourself. With a medium- to large-sized team, there may well be a 'co-ordinator' or 'rally manager' (as opposed to team manager), who to some extent will take the load off you with regard to the pre-event movements and ferry and hotel bookings, as well as controlling service matters during the event. If you're lucky enough to have such a person with your team, he becomes your link man with the rest of the outfit, but even so you cannot opt out of relating directly to the mechanics and other workers. This means getting on first name terms with them all, otherwise when you need a job doing in a service area, you are in the embarrassing situation of calling out, 'Hey, you', which is hardly conducive to a good rapport, or indeed getting your request attended to at all.

Early season

In the early stages you should be spending quite some time down at the workshops where the car is prepared, if only to sort out your 'office' in the manner already described in Chapter 7. While the mechanics might not relish the extra work you're bringing them, they will come to recognize your commitment and dedication to the cause. In due course, especially if you're taking the trouble to spend time with them and appreciate their problems, that should translate into acceptance and respect, particularly if they see that you're also doing a good job on events.

Briefing

Even if your team is a small one, you should have some sort of pre-event service briefing. In theory, the service schedule should tell everyone where they should be and when, how much fuel to put in, what tyres to fit and so on. I have to admit, with regret, that not every mechanic reads the schedule as it's intended to be read (we'll look at the schedule itelf later in this chapter), so you need the briefing just to drive home certain key points as you see them. Even if the team has a co-ordinator, the co-driver should still attend the briefing and contribute to it. Tell them about the event format, the time penalties and the maximum lateness. If you have identified what you see as a key service point, perhaps where access is difficult, at which timing is tight, or between two long or difficult stages, it does no harm to go over the arrangements and the problems of this particular point. Talk about the tyres, which types you're likely to use where, where the 'chase car' (if any) should keep a low profile, which vehicle is going to carry the spotlamps and what should happen in case of retirement. Make any points which

Below left *A co-ordinator is very useful. Here Alistair Roberts and Team Manager David Ewles check the stage times, work list and service time available with the author after a tough stage on the Scottish Rally, 1990. (Kolczak.)*

Below right *A pre-event service briefing is essential for all the team. The author says his 'two penn'orth' prior to the Scottish Rally, 1990. (Kolczak.)*

you feel are important, but do keep your briefing brief—
mechanics' span of attention for such affairs can be somewhat short.

On events

'Doing a good job on events' is not the same in a rally mechanic's eyes as in a driver's eyes. The criteria are quite different,
even though they may overlap in certain respects. The mechanics will be looking for good information before the event
starts—their maps, their service schedule, their tyre loads
where applicable. They'll expect an accurate fuel calculation—
they won't be impressed if you're asking for a full tank all the
time, even less if you run out of fuel, so do your calculations
carefully. Get the mechanics to provide you with a fuel con-
sumption figure for stages and for road sections, make your
calculations, then add a reserve of about 10 litres/2 gallons.

In the service areas, or preferably before (if you have a
radio), they'd like a concise list of work you or your driver would
like to have done, as well as some warning of your impending
arrival. Next they'll need an accurate estimate of the service
time available to them, so they can decide whether they have
time to complete a job or not, and so they can organize their
priorities. Wherever you arrange for them to service, it's a
good idea to have some sort of identifying service board (so
long as they don't leave it behind when they leave) or flashing
light system on the 'barge' so that you can find them easily. In
a crowded service area, one mechanic should always be positioned at the entrance to point or lead you in the right
direction, otherwise you will waste valuable time hunting round
for the 'barge'.

Non-timed service

When it comes to estimating the available service time on road
sections (where permissible), you should already know from
your pre-event work on the road book (and so should the
mechanics, if they've actually read their service schedule)
what this ought to be, but it may have been increased if you've
made better time than expected on the road section, or
decreased if the traffic's been bad or if you've had some
problems with the car. Always check the time available and
confirm it to the mechanics. Don't be over-cautious in the
calculation, for that will tempt them to put off a job that they
could well have had time to fix, nor over-optimistic, as that
could lead to lateness at the next control. However, most

Above *Non-timed service may be alongside the public highway, especially abroad.* (Kolczak.)

Right *Frenzied service action on Safari, as TTE mechanics change Bjorn Waldegaard's gearbox. On this event, most service time comes out of competitive road section time.* (Lodge.)

Below *That was a bit tight... Luis Moya dives for the control having just arrived within his minute on 1000 Lakes Rally, 1991.* (Kolczak.)

Left *Booking into a timed service area.* (Lodge.)

Below right *Try to keep the service point clear for the mechanics to work. Non-essential personnel (including co-drivers) should not obstruct the areas between the cars and the service vans.* (Kolczak.)

Below *Service areas can be very crowded places. Always check your route to the out control.* (Lodge.)

co-drivers—myself included—generally keep the odd minute 'up their sleeve', just in case, and how often I've been glad of that when we've just scraped into a time control with only a few seconds to spare without penalty.

Timed service

Quite a lot of smaller rallies, and several big ones, have timed service areas where you clock in, take service and clock out again. Here it's easier to be precise about your service time, but remember these areas tend to be crowded so progress within them can be rather slow. Driving quickly in a service area is dangerous—someone could easily get run over—so while the car is in service, check the way to the time control and make allowances with your available time. Obviously, the nearer your service location is to the exit time control, the easier it is to be precise about your service time. Encourage your mechanics to set up near to the 'out' control, but clearly not every team can do this, otherwise the exit would become choked.

In service

Once the service work is under way, you should keep out of the way, as you're likely to impede the mechanics' work. Not only you, but other co-drivers, press, friends and 'hangers-on' may come to speak with you, further adding to the impediment of mechanical activity. The very worst place to stand is the area between the rally car and the service 'barge' and if you receive

Above left *You can use the service time to catch up on the stage times of your rivals. (Lodge.)*

Above right *If the weather's bad, you can always sit in the service van, have a cup of tea and raid the mechanics' lunch boxes. (Hodson/CCC.)*

Below *Anxious moments... Team Manager David Ewles double checks with the author as time starts to get tight for completion of the service work, Circuit of Ireland,1990. (Kolczak.)*

a rap on the arm with a crowbar or have your toes run over by a jack, you only have yourself to blame. You can use this service time to go and check other crews' stage times, but always keep an eye on progress of your own service. If the weather's bad, you can always sit in the cab of the service van, as this will probably be unoccupied, and you can raid the mechanics' lunch box (they will not love you for this). Some indication of the passage of time will be appreciated by the mechanics, particularly if they're involved in a big job, so '10 minutes', '5 minutes', then '3', '2' and '1 minute to go' calls are in order, but don't overdo the drama or you'll only panic them into errors or forgetting to do up important nuts and bolts. If you get too excited in a service area and start screaming and shouting, you'll upset the mechanics and probably the driver too, with the result that he'll be too 'pumped up' for the next stage and may well make a mistake and go off. So again, keep as calm as you can. Finally, when it's time to leave, someone should guide you out of the service area.

Morale

If time permits, keep the service crew informed about your times and progress; sometimes service crews feel they're being treated on the 'mushroom principle'—keep them in the dark and cover them with manure. So to alleviate this problem, do let them know how things are going, how the driver is

Someone should also guide you out when the work is done. (Kolczak.)

driving, how the stages are working out, any amusing or dramatic incidents and so on. They're only human and like to hear such things from yourself, rather than read about it in next week's *Motoring News*. Also, if they've done a good job and kept you in the rally without penalty, don't be afraid to thank them at the time or over the radio once you've cleared the control; much as you would like to have your own efforts appreciated (fat chance), so would the mechanics like to know that someone takes an interest in their work. The next time you want something, they'll remember little things like that.

Service schedule

The job of rally management could occupy quite a large space in this book, but as we're primarily concerned with the co-driver's duties, let's look at a service schedule that you might prepare yourself. Many people make the mistake of thinking that a service schedule is only for the service crews and then wonder why it appears so complicated or contains so much information. The answer is that although primarily aimed at the service crew, it is in fact the whole team's 'bible' for the complete event. As well as the mechanics, the co-driver and occasionally the driver need to refer to it, while in a bigger team, the 'chase car', the co-ordinator, the team manager, the engineer, the motorhome crew, the press officer and the tyre company also need to draw on it for information. So people need to be able to select the pieces of information which are important to their own function, hence the diversity of the information.

Planning

In the planning stage you will have already worked out things like service time and fuel quantity; for the service schedule, in addition, you need to calculate the ability of your service crews to achieve their various points on time. It's no good setting them impossible averages and then wondering why they're late or miss the point altogether. On a small event, all the service points are usually easily achieved by one service vehicle.

For a small team on a big event, you have to be selective of the important places where you must have service; some stages you may have no service at all. For a bigger team, it's a question of making the best use of your resources without overstretching them.

A loaded service van won't often average much more than 30

The service schedule is the team's 'bible'—different sections have relevance to different people in the team.

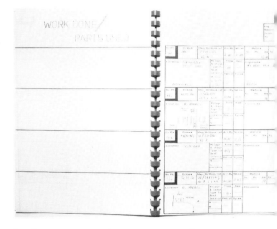

mph (less on country lanes) and these men have to pack up after the rally car has left and get set up at the next point, all of which takes time. Being large vehicles, they are more affected by traffic jams than a nimble car. Look carefully at their routings, calculate the distances and make adjustments to the schedule. It is better to have an unambitious schedule which you're sure will work, than a chancy one which might lead to your going out of the event. I find that the 1:250,000 series maps are excellent for service planning, because they give you a broader view of the rally area and enable you to plot vehicle movements more effectively.

Chase cars

If you're running a 'chase car', do understand the risks of taking service from it. On smaller events it's questionable whether you need one, but if you decide to make use of it, understand that you may attract penalties if caught taking service in an illegal location. Your philosophy may well be that it's worth taking the chance, especially as, if you didn't, you'd be out of the rally anyway. But don't say I didn't warn you. On bigger events, some organizers have become a little more tolerant of 'chase cars'; some provide sections of route after a stage for these vehicles only. After all, their event is better off if cars can be kept in the rally. Again, planning of the 'chase car' routing will need some care and attention from you. Don't have them rushing about too much otherwise they'll probably cause an accident on the narrow lanes they may have to use.

Layout

To provide a reasonable level of information your schedule

Left *Refuelling is an important job. Make sure the mechanic responsible understands the routine... and, please, no smoking.* (Kolczak.)

Below right *Tyres can present a bewildering choice. Here slicks, mixed surface and a variety of gravel patterns and sizes are on view.* (Lodge.)

should show most, if not all, of the following:
Service point number
Location—name of place, map ref, road book ref.
Diagram of service point, if applicable
Vehicle(s) in attendance
Due time of first car
Service time
Before or after which stage
Before or after which time control
How long the next stage(s) before next service
How much fuel to be in the tank
Tyres to be fitted
Service vehicle routing and distance
Special comments, e,g, fit lights, narrow access
How much of this you include will depend on your team resources and what you feel to be necessary. For a small team you can certainly trim this down to avoid an overkill situation. You can use an existing format, or design your own; it doesn't matter so long as it's reasonably clear and logical. If however you find yourself being asked lots of basic questions by the service crew during the event, then either you are not putting enough basic information in, or they're not reading it.

This can be a problem; even though, for example, it says 'leave with 30 litres in the fuel tank', the mechanic whose responsibility it is to refill the car still asks the question 'How much fuel?'. If this sort of thing happens more than a couple of times, have a quiet word with him on his own, explain that the service schedule is just as much for his benefit as everyone else's and suggest he has a quick check of the scheduled fuel figure before his next service point, then looks at the fuel gauge when you arrive. Again, don't be heavy-handed or you'll destroy his self-confidence. Perhaps at the service briefing earlier you could stress how important it is that everyone reads, understands and acts upon the service schedule. It's important that you can entrust such jobs to the service crew so that you can concentrate on your other duties, even though ultimately you will have to check that the task has been carried out.

Tyres

The most critical factor in rallying has to be the tyres. As I stated earlier, the choice may be the driver's province, but as the co-driver you need to understand the workings of the rubberwear. At times the choice can be staggering, but you have to come to terms with that choice, so that you can make the various logistical calculations of what tyres must be on which service vehicle, where and when. Each tyre manufacturer's range goes from skinny snow tyres, through narrow and wide gravel tyres with a plethora of patterns, constructions, sizes and compounds, to mixed-surface tyres and finally racing tyres, also with a bewildering choice of patterns and compounds.

With a small team on a small budget the only problem will be persuading the limited number of tyres you have to get you to

the finish, using and re-using your best part-worns and hoping for no punctures. With a bigger operation the choice expands, sometimes to the point where it's not always easy to end up with the right choice at the right service point. So you need some sort of tyre plan. Frankly, it quite often doesn't work out right, so do it in pencil at first on a trial-and-error basis in order

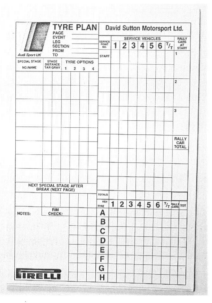

Above left *To ensure that the right tyres are on the right van in the right place at the right time, you need some sort of tyre plan.*

Above *From the tyre plan you can produce a load list.*

Left *Tyre warmers (even for gravel tyres) are essential for larger teams as they search for any fractional advantage. This is Lancia in Argentina, 1991. (Lodge.)*

that you can make modifications. The restricting factors will be the number of tyres, the number of rims, the number of service vehicles and the carrying capacity of those service vehicles. From your tyre plan, you can then produce a load list for each vehicle.

With still bigger teams, the whole complexity of the tyre situation means that separate tyre trucks have to be deployed to carry the selection of rubber, as well as tyre warmers and the generators to drive them, since the service vans no longer have the capacity to transport such a range or quantity. But let's not worry about that now—just concentrate on understanding the usage of the various tyres you do have and on making sure they get to the right place at the right time.

Wrong choice

The other problem with so wide a tyre choice is to try to ensure that your choice is a correct one. Now this really is primarily down to the driver, as his feel for the car and conditions, as well as his previous experience, will generally dictate that choice. If you develop a good understanding of tyres, you can become a useful 'sounding board' for your driver, however; after each stage, discuss the tyre choice and see if you're both happy with the tyres you've just used.

If not, and especially if the service crew are not expecting your new choice, try to give them warning over the radio to have the alternatives ready. They should have pressure-checked all the tyres anyway, but a radio call will initiate this action as well as prompt them to get the tyres down off the roof rack and ready for use.

Inevitably, and especially on tarmac where the choice is more critical, you will on occasions find yourselves on the wrong tyres. You may be using slicks and then it rains; you put on wets and it dries out—you know the situation well. Simo Lampinen, the great Finnish driver, once said of such a rally, 'My tyre choice has been like a watch that has stopped—only twice a day has it been right.' Coping with such conditions is down to the driver, but an experienced co-driver, with one eye on the weather, can often point him in the right direction on tyre selection, though at times it may feel rather like Russian Roulette.

Two-way radio

Mention of the radio prompts me to say a few words about this aspect of communications. Certainly you can manage without a radio, but many teams, even small teams, seem to have them nowadays. There are many ways that a radio can be useful; we've just touched on the situation of an unexpected tyre choice, but there are plenty of others that you will find: a problem on a stage, or indeed anywhere?—your chase car can perhaps render assistance, when otherwise you might go out of the rally. A description of where the service van is located?—this saves valuable service time. The list of service jobs?—this enables the service crew to plan their actions. A blockage on a road section?—forewarned by radio, you might find an alternative way round. A police radar trap?—I believe warning of this is classed as 'obstructing the police in the execution of their duty'. You will find plenty more uses. As in military situations, good communications can win the battle.

There are attendant problems, I must admit. You will need a licence for your radio, though this is not difficult to obtain. The range of the sets is generally none too good: if hills or buildings obtrude, you might struggle to make contact. If you've got flat country and 'line of sight' you can communicate, otherwise there's a frustrating lack of connection at many times, as rallies generally take place in hilly regions. Interference can be a problem, particularly in towns or near military installations. You may be sharing the same channel with other crews, or even with people not connected with the rally. This can lead to some very strange or very amusing conversations at times, but it won't help your rally effort. Rally organizers have been known to equip their Judges of Fact with radio scanners, so if you've just announced that you'd like to do a bit of illegal servicing in the car park of the 'Jolly Farmer' pub, don't be surprised if you're joined there by a couple of burly chaps with official armbands.

There are in-car problems as well. Inevitably there will be times when you forget to turn the radio off for a stage and you become distracted by other people's ramblings. Equally, there will be times when you give a long set of instructions over the radio and wonder why no-one is answering you, only to discover that you haven't switched the set on, or are using the wrong channel, or you've got the volume turned right down and can't hear their response. We've all done it, believe me. One of the worst things you can do—and this applies to your service crews as well—is to 'sit on the mike', which means that you transmit inadvertently because the microphone has fallen out of its clip and is jammed in the 'transmit' position. This has the effect of obliterating all radio communication and is extremely annoying to those who suffer as a result. Don't forget that others may hear what you have to say, so be careful if you wish

To make the most of the two-way radio you should speak clearly, keeping the message brief and to the point. (Lodge.)

to discuss something confidential or sensitive and, needless to say, keep your language clean and inoffensive.

The first time you install a radio in the car, it will be like a new toy and you will play with it just like a kid, using it excessively and unnecessarily. Soon, however, you should settle down to using it properly, i.e. sparingly and concisely. Keep conversations short and to the point and only speak when necessary. Don't get over-excited about something—if you shout you'll just distort everything. And don't criticize someone over the radio—save it for a face-to-face meeting later.

While I don't suggest that you go quite as far as to use pilot terms for radio talk, there are lessons to be learned from the aviation world; those people depend on good radio communications, so they generally get it right. On this basis, a typical Toyota GB radio conversation would begin like this:

'Tango One—this is Tango David' (which means that David Llewellin or Phil Short wishes to speak to Tango One, a service vehicle).

'Go ahead, Tango David, this is Tango One' (this translates as Tango One can hear and wishes David/Phil to pass his message).

Thereafter, in the interests of time you can drop the 'Tango' call sign and speak informally but a little slower and clearer than if you were discussing face to face. The word 'Over' at the end of your message signifies to the other party that you've finished speaking and he can now reply.

It's always a good idea to announce over the radio when you're about to start a stage, so that the rest of the team cuts the talking in case you need to transmit an urgent message mid-stage. Also, make a call about two minutes before you arrive at the service point, so that the crew are expecting you and can direct you in. If you have a short message which is addressed to no particular vehicle and expecting no reply, the call might be: 'This is Tango David, finished stage three—no problems'. That way you are keeping the airwaves free for more important talk. Always remember to be brief and to the point—don't ramble on. Wait until the other person finishes his message before replying, otherwise you'll 'trample' over him and neither of you will understand a word. When the conversation comes to an end, please, please don't say 'Over and Out' as they do in films. 'Over' means over to you, i.e. expecting a response; 'Out' means the conversation is finished. So if you think about it, 'Over and Out' is contradictory and meaningless, even if it does make you feel like a celluloid wartime ace.

The radio is an important tool in your job; with a little care and practice you can become proficient at using it properly. You can effectively run the team from your seat inside the car, providing you've got good communications and the rest of the team also learns to be cool, calm and collected when 'on air'.

De-brief

My final suggestion on service matters is to try to arrange a debriefing session, either immediately after the rally (while things are fresh in people's minds) or within a few days (when everyone has had a chance to cool down). That way, problems can be aired, discussed and hopefully resolved before the next event. That is the only way for the team to progress and overcome difficulties and disagreements. It also allows you to say 'thank you', which is the least the service guys deserve.

Chapter 10

Problems

If you haven't realized it by now, you will soon come to
understand that a lot of rallying is about solving problems.
How to go rallying in the first place, how to find the money, how
to find success, how to move up the ladder—these are some of
the general problems that you will already have had to contend
with. What we're going to look at in this chapter, however, are
the more specific problems, especially those concerning the
co-driver. They may also concern others in the team, but they
are problems with which the co-driver will have to learn how to
deal. Clearly, there are so many things that can go wrong—
some serious, some annoying, some amusing—that I cannot
cover them all. Nor can I, like some 'agony aunt', claim to have
the answers to all of them, though from my own experiences I
can perhaps point you in the right direction. We can divide our
problems into pre-event, on-event and post-event.

Pre-event problems

We've already covered the situation of a reserve entry and
hopefully converting it into a full entry. However, let's say
you've got an entry but the car preparation is getting behind
schedule, what should you do? If the problem is parts availability and there's no sign of a solution in time, then pull the
entry out as soon as you can—that way you may recover most
of the entry fee. If the problem is man hours, then get your
driver to take stock of the situation and decide if he's really
going to make it in time. Perhaps some sort of cut-off date for
a near-completion would help and if you haven't achieved it,
again, withdraw the entry. The earlier you can do that, the
more chance you have of a refund, especially if there's a
reserve list. However, the resourcefulness and determination
of drivers and mechanics will often bring about a completion

Bigger events have a Parc Fermé. Quite often the rally car can be delivered there by a mechanic, not necessarily by the crew. However, when it's your time to go to the car (10 minutes before your start time), make sure you don't turn up late. (Lodge.)

against the odds, so you need to guard against premature pessimism.

I mention these problems because almost certainly it will be the co-driver who has to make the call to the organizers informing them of the non-start. In fact, if there is some doubt about your starting, it might help future relations if you keep the organizers aware of your difficulties. Like you, they don't appreciate nasty surprises. Don't just fail to turn up without an explanation; that's very bad manners. Next time you want an entry from these organizers, they will remember that. If the team is running late, hindered by last-minute preparation problems or perhaps by severe traffic delays, you may be able to get a later scrutineering time, if you ring up and ask. In extreme circumstances, on a smaller event, you might even get a later start time, but clearly that could be detrimental to your performance.

One self-inflicted problem can be late arrival at the start/restart. Rallying is punctuated with stories of crews who have turned up late because they missed a bulletin about a revised time, or they didn't allow sufficient time or got stuck in the traffic or overslept or whatever. So get a good alarm clock (never, in my experience, are hotel alarm calls to be relied upon), do allow plenty of time to get down to the start and always make a confirmatory check of your published start time. If a Parc Fermé is involved, you are allowed to enter 10 minutes before your due start time and not before. However, you should go in on your 10 minutes, because that way you'll know as soon as possible if there's a problem with starting the car. Remember, you cannot work on the car in Parc Fermé, but you can push it out and work on it once clear of the control.

On-event problems

It's here where you will get the most problems, simply because of the nature of the competition. Everybody is stressed—

driver, co-driver, mechanics, marshals, organizers—and consequently mistakes are made. Likewise the equipment is under stress; the car, its various components and the tyres are likely to give trouble.

Marshalling problems

Marshalling errors are unfortunately common, even on big events. Organizers find it hard to get good, experienced marshals for all of their controls; consequently some may be manned by less knowledgeable people who don't understand the regulations or who haven't been properly briefed or who don't know how to deal with an unexpected situation. That could work to your advantage, but more usually it's to your disadvantage, so always check, for instance, that the correct figures have been written in the correct place on your time card. If you leave the control and find the problem shortly afterwards, then if time permits you should go back (without the rally car re-entering the control) and get it corrected. Similarly, if you 'missed' a poorly sited passage control, it's better to swallow your pride, go back and get it sorted there and then, as you're unlikely to resolve the matter at the finish.

I once had a situation where we finished a stage on 20h–20m–17s. For the start of the subsequent road section the marshal wrote a plausible 20h–17m (instead of 20h–20m), and as the stage card was removed at a passage control soon after the finish, I didn't spot the error, so with a, say, 30 minute road section to follow I appeared to be scheduled to book in at 20h–47m, rather than the correct 20h–50m. Result—three minutes' earliness penalty. As the original error was that of the marshal, you might feel that the problem would be later corrected. Had it made any difference to the result, I might have been inclined to protest, but the rules do state that the onus rests with the competitor to ensure that the entries on the time card are correct. You have been warned.

To be honest, quite a few of the marshalling problems occur for the first few cars (especially car 1) when the officials haven't quite got their act together. For the later cars, they've got into their stride. Errors of the one minute discrepancy are now fortunately rare, due to the digital watches in use, but sometimes the marshal can inadvertently stop the clock by allowing the button to bang against his chest, so always keep an eye on your own timepiece to see that times coincide.

Disputes

If you get into a dispute with a marshal, do try to be firm but polite. Don't forget, these people are unpaid volunteers who put in a lot of time and effort so that you can have your day's sport; there's no point in being heavily abusive or unpleasant. If necessary, and if time permits, produce your set of regulations which might cover the mistake he's making. If not, make a report and hand it in at the next suitable control; this could help to resolve the problem later. Remember, the clock is still running all the time you're having your 'discussion' with the marshal, so make sure you don't end up late at the next control as a result.

Road section problems

Particularly on bigger events, there can be problems of congestion on the roads, caused by the sheer volume of traffic connected with the rally, be it spectator traffic or service vehicles. A thoughtful organizer might foresee this and take competitors via a less obvious but possibly longer and more tortuous route, to avoid the potential problem area. Not all organizers are so thoughtful, nor can they foresee some unexpected blockage such as a road accident, newly-commenced roadworks or impromptu protests by anti-rally factions. Your pre-event planning should have thrown up the more obvious problem points, but what do you do when you're caught by the unexpected blockage of a road section?

Firstly, you should have the relevant map to hand so that you can weigh up your alternatives. You may have no alternative but to sit it out and wait for the blockage to clear; assuming a good number of other competitors are similarly afflicted, there is a good chance that any penalties will be cancelled. On the other hand, it may be possible to do a short detour and regain the rally route a little further on. Only the map will tell you this, but make sure you don't drive through a 'no go area' or miss a control. Strictly speaking, you are obliged to stick to the rally route and you can be penalized for deviating from it. In a blockage situation however, most organizers would accept that you acted reasonably and therefore not apply any penalty. Clearly, if there is a serious accident and you can render assistance, perhaps with your first aid kit or fire extinguisher or by using your radio, it's your duty to do so, regardless of your schedule. Again, the organizers, not to mention the authorities, would look favourably on such action.

Don't get drawn into a long detour that will have you struggling against the clock. Quite often, in my experience, these blockages have a tendency to clear quicker than you expect, so with a little patience it may well turn out well. Nevertheless, such occurrences are nerve-wracking times for co-drivers and a quickening of the road section pace may be required to achieve your next control on time. For this reason, if your service point is some way from the time control, you should aim to have a few minutes 'up your sleeve' when you leave non-timed service, to guard against the unexpected.

Police

Talk of quickening the pace brings us to the possibility of being stopped by the police. It is a sad fact that most (though not all) British police forces do not have an enlightened view about rallying. Rather than help the rally along by improving traffic flow, many officers are content to allow a problem to develop and then jump on the competitor or service vehicle that steps out of line. On the other hand, not all rally people are good, careful or considerate road users and there is no doubt that some rally drivers abuse the privilege of having a powerful car in their hands. None of us is above the law and rally crews cannot expect any sort of preferential treatment, at least not in this country. The upshot of this is that, as I mentioned earlier, you can expect an increased police presence on road sections, particularly on the bigger events. Public opinion in certain areas may demand that the police enforce, for example, a speed limit along a particular stretch of road, to appease residents who have in the past complained about rally cars 'racing' through the area. Unfortunately, not everyone understands the technicalities of our sport and that road sections are non-competitive. It's quite likely in this situation that the police will catch far more locals than rally cars.

One of your tasks should be to keep your driver calm on the road, saving the aggression for the stages. Educate him into the keeping of a reasonable speed; don't be afraid to slow him down or to point out some approaching road hazard or speed limit. For all your precautions however, there may be an occasion when your driver is stopped by the police for some offence. Quite often an apology will see you on your way, but if the officer feels so inclined there may be a report. There's no point in either of you losing your cool—that will only exacerbate the situation. Just bite your tongue, let the formalities take place and then you can proceed on your way without further ado. Remember, the organizers' clock is still running. You are however obliged to make a report of the incident to the organizers at the next suitable control, or at the finish. It may be that you will be subject to further penalties from the organizers, but it still remains your duty to make that report.

On-stage problems

This is where most of your difficulties will arise, when you're in the thick of the action. How you handle them will determine how much time you lose or whether you get out of the stage at all.

Punctures

Perhaps the most common problem is a puncture, brought about by the roughness of the roads or a driver error—clipping

Left *Punctures are a common problem. You should both know and practise your individual tasks and just get on with them without panic.* (Lodge.)

Below *If you stop near a group of spectators, they can perhaps lift the car, obviating the need for the jack and (hopefully) speeding up the change.* (Lodge.)

a rock, putting a wheel in a ditch, brushing a bank or whatever. If the stage is short, you won't have to stop and change. If you have a few miles to go to the finish, it will depend on several factors whether you need to stop. Generally a front puncture is more serious than a rear, especially in a car with driven front wheels. In my experience, seven miles is about the critical point: less than this and you'll probably lose less time by running out; more than this, you'll lose less time by stopping and changing. But this is just an estimated figure; it will vary according to the car you have, the tyre being used and the surface of the stage. A rear puncture, particularly in a front wheel drive car can be left for longer. Your ability to change the wheel quickly also has a bearing on what you decide to do.

Ideally, you should practise a wheel change back at base. Time yourselves from sitting in the car, belted and helmeted, to back in the same position having changed the wheel. Anything over three minutes in these circumstances is very poor: more practice required. On a stage, conditions will be harder for you, especially in the dark or in bad weather. Work out who is going to do the various jobs: extract the jack, jack up the car, extract the wheelbrace, undo the wheel nuts, extract the spare wheel, remove and stow the old wheel, fit the new, tighten the nuts, release the jack, stow all the gear, etc., etc. Discussing who should do what when changing in the stage is going to slow you down; you should both know your jobs and just get on with them. Sometimes the work can be speeded up if you stop by some spectators; on a light car, there might be enough people to lift the car so you don't need the jack. Also try to stop in a safe place, which allows you room to work without impeding or being impeded by the next cars, and where there is a firm base, otherwise the jack may sink into the soft ground and fail to lift the car. If it's a night-time stage, you'll need a torch. Some crews are put out of rallies because they discover at the time of their mid-stage change that either the jack doesn't work or the wheelbrace is the wrong size for the nuts. A pre-rally check will avoid this.

On the Ulster Rally in 1990, David Llewellin and I changed a punctured wheel and lost only 1m 52s to the fastest time; we were almost as proud of that as winning the rally. One thing which David is always careful about is to fasten up his belts properly after a mid-stage stop; it's easy to be tempted to leave this job, but it's quite common for drivers to go off the road soon after a puncture, perhaps trying too hard to make up lost time, so do up your belts, both of you, before you set off. You'll struggle to fasten them on the move, though you should be able to reconnect the intercom as you get going if you've

Above left *You can quite often drive out on a puncture, so long as the driver doesn't 'load up' the punctured side. (Lodge.)*

Above right *Once clear of the stage finish control, you can change the tyre. Here Robbie Philpott goes to work on the rear wheel of Kenny McKinstry's Sierra Cosworth. (Lodge.)*

taped the sockets to your belts as suggested.

If you decide to continue to the end, the driver can help the situation by not 'loading up' the corner with the puncture. So, with a left-hand puncture he should take it easy on right-handers. He may feel this is costing more time, but in fact, if he disintegrates the tyre or causes it to roll off the rim, he's going to lose much more, as well as cause greater mechanical damage, so a bit of caution is required. Keep an eye open for the car on the minute behind you: he'll not be happy to be baulked, unseen by you, until the finish. Finally, when you get to the stage end, try to get the car clear of the stop line before changing the wheel, so as not to impede the running of the stage.

Water problems

Water can cause all sorts of problems on a stage. It can drown the engine, either through the induction system or by fouling up the electrics. If your car is prone to this, you should apply extra waterproofing measures before going into a stage containing a known ford. The driver's technique will help: blasting flat out through a deep watersplash may look good on the photos, but if the engine takes in water and you lose time, it's all a bit pointless. The sheer weight of water can also smash your lights.

The water can also cause your windscreen to mist up heavily. If you have a heated front screen, you need to have this switched on a few minutes before hitting the water. Failing that, turn on the fan to full in the demist position. I suggest you put a note to remind you of this in your road book or in the pace notes. I would also insert the word 'wipers' in my pace notes before the watersplash, so that neither of us was groping for the switch while the screen was covered in mud and water.

Mechanical problems

I cannot list all the technical problems which might afflict you, so you and your driver will have to take each one on its merits. Generally speaking, if the car has a problem but still runs, it's better not to stop, unless you know (perhaps from past experience) exactly what the problem is and it's something you can fix quickly, like a detached plug lead. If the problem stops the car, then obviously you must try to fix it to get going. Quite often, electrical problems are the cause, so know your way around the fuses and connections. If the throttle cable breaks, it's not unknown for one of the crew to operate the throttle from under the bonnet while the other one drives, or, in the case of a major suspension failure, for the co-driver to sit on the diametrically opposite end to keep the damaged corner off the deck. On some events, however, there may be a penalty,

Below left *In extremes, someone sometimes has to take drastic measures. Here Juha Kankkunen operates the broken throttle while Juha Piironen drives. 1000 Lakes Rally, 1990. (Selden.)*

Below right *If you can fix the mechanical problem quickly, then sometimes that's better than struggling to the end. Perhaps this driver should be careful of subsequent cars passing close by him. (Kolczak.)*

possibly exclusion, for doing this. As I say, you will have to find the solution to each individual problem as best you can.

Off the road

Accept the fact that this is going to happen to you more than a few times in your rallying career. Ninety-nine times out of a hundred, you won't be hurt, so the question is, can you get back on the road? Sometimes, the car will just drive out, backwards or forwards, especially if it's four wheel drive. If not, then maybe some spectatators nearby (they usually have a 'nose' for such places) will push you out. Failing that, it's time for you to get out and start shoving. Make sure all your paperwork is properly stowed; a lost time card, road book or pace notes will probably eliminate you anyway. Open the windows; this gives you another area of purchase and improves communication with the driver. Try to get a good footing and really put your back into a good shove, in concert with an application of power by the driver.

If that doesn't work, see what's stopping the car from moving—perhaps a tree stump or rocks or logs underneath. Maybe you can move them, but be careful, if the car is in a precarious position, that it doesn't topple over onto you. Quite often, more damage is done to a car in getting it out than was caused by the original accident, and it's easy to break it in this situation, putting you out altogether. So don't rush things; take

Below left *If your driver's trying hard, going off is an occupational hazard. Most times you'll end up back on the road.* (Lodge.)

Below right *But occasionally you will get the feeling that things have got beyond recall.* (Kolczak.)

This page *A roll is not as bad as it looks. Sometimes, if you stay put, the spectators will have you back on your wheels and away in no time. Colin McRae on his way to winning the 1989 Trackrod Forest Stages.* (Lodge.)

stock of the situation and think about the best way to get out of your predicament.

If spectatators arrive, having heard you go off, do try to organize them into helping you back on. When we went off in Ireland once and landed on top of a bank, two groups of spectators started pushing from both ends of the car, until I suggested they concentrate their efforts in just the one direction. You can also orchestrate the pushing and shoving with a lusty '3-2-1-Push' exhortation. It's surprising sometimes how much you can achieve with a concerted effort. Send the least solid citizen back down the road to warn subsequent crews, otherwise another competitor may well join you off the road.

Roll

This is not quite as bad as it sounds. Generally, if a car rolls it loses its momentum gradually, rather than in a sudden impact. So the damage may well be relatively superficial. My recommendation in this upside-down situation is to stay put in your seat, for the spectators will probably have you back on your wheels shortly. On the 1000 Lakes Rally once, Markku Alen rolled and lost just 12 seconds to fastest time. A roll can be a little disorientating, but if you remain in position, even upside down, you can still relate to your 'office' and leave the driver to organize the spectators, where necessary. If you have to get out, do it carefully; as you undo the belts, you will end up in a heap on the roof. Also, there may be broken glass about, so try to avoid lacerating yourself. The doors may be stuck, so you may need to exit via a window. All part of life's rich tapestry.

If you do have to get out, it may have to be via a window, as the doors may be jammed. Beware of broken glass. (Kolczak.)

Retirement

It could be that despite all your efforts, you cannot regain the road or the car has broken down totally. As soon as you reach this decision point, you need to find your OK board and warning triangle. Put the OK board somewhere on the car, if visible to other crews (this is so that the marshals at the finish don't get over-concerned about you), and set up the warning triangle at a suitable distance before the point where your car is, to warn following drivers. Put it where it won't get knocked over, otherwise the damage to your car is likely to be added to when others, not forewarned, join you in your unexpected location.

If you're not far from the beginning or end of the stage, perhaps one of you can walk out. This will get precise news to

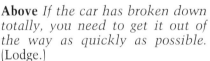

Above *If the car has broken down totally, you need to get it out of the way as quickly as possible.* (Lodge.)

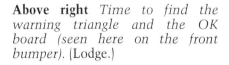

Above right *Time to find the warning triangle and the OK board (seen here on the front bumper).* (Lodge.)

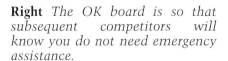

Right *The OK board is so that subsequent competitors will know you do not need emergency assistance.*

167

the marshals and perhaps via a fellow competitor, you can get a message to your service crew to come and retrieve you. The organizers usually have vehicles capable of towing you out, but if something more substantial is required, perhaps the crew member who goes out can start to get that organized. However, one of you should stay with the car, as unfortunately it's not unknown for an unattended rally car to have parts and equipment stolen from it. Incidentally, you must still hand in your accident declaration form at the finish; the organizers may also like to know the reason for your retirement.

Serious accident

God forbid that this should happen, but occasionally it does. If one of you is injured, the other should get the SOS or Red Cross board and display it to the next competitor, who will then get a message to the stage finish or next radio point as soon as possible. This will activate the stage safety plan, which hopefully will bring medical assistance shortly. Until help arrives, the best plan is to keep the injured person still; sometimes injuries, especially spinal injuries or broken limbs, can be worsened by trying to move someone out of a car. If he's not in immediate danger, leave him where he is until the experts arrive, but keep him warm to guard against the effects of shock. It's best not to try to remove his helmet as this too can aggravate injuries still further. In your preparations, it might help for both of you to learn the basics of first aid. In my

If you do need emergency assistance, display the SOS board.

168

distant Boy Scouting days I learnt about stopping bleeding from arteries, mouth-to-mouth resuscitation and so on, but thankfully, I've never had to put the knowledge to actual use.

Fire

Of course, if there is a real risk of fire, then you must try to move, but carefully, the injured person. Even if there are no injuries, the car's fire extinguishing system (which should be 'armed' as soon as the event is underway) should be activated where necessary, but if it's only a small fire then the hand-held will do. Turn off the electrics with the master switch, because not only does this reduce a possible cause of fire, but also cuts the fuel pumps which may still be pushing petrol around the system. As many of our rallies take place in forests, the prospect of a forest fire started by a burning rally car is not one which would endear us to the Forestry Commission, so make sure your extingushers work (and what's more, that you know how to use them) and have them checked regularly and replenished when necessary.

Post-event problems

It would be wrong of me to try to turn you into the rallying equivalent of the 'barrack room lawyer'. Rallying is a sport and therefore to be enjoyed. Clearly, that enjoyment diminishes if everyone reaches for their Blue Book every time something untoward occurs. As you will know from your study of the Blue Book, the regulations are plentiful; it would seem almost impossible to avoid falling foul of them at some point. There will regrettably come a time when you need to have recourse to the regulations to resolve a particular problem. If you feel that something incorrect has occurred to your detriment, or to the unfair benefit of a rival, then quite often a quiet word with the Clerk of the Course, Competitor Liaison Officer or other senior official may resolve the problem. Failing that, an official 'Query Form', outlining your complaint, may eradicate the error—ideal for timing errors perhaps. But what do you do if that doesn't bring satisfaction?

Protests

First you have to look carefully at your situation. Will a protest actually achieve anything worthwhile? Does it make any difference to you whether you are 47th or 42nd, or 9th or 7th in class? In this case, I would suggest you make your point of view known and then avoid what could be classed as a frivolous protest. If, on the other hand, things are more serious, then you first need to take a good, hard look at your case. Go somewhere quiet, away from the scrum at the Rally HQ and talk over the situation with your driver and possibly the rest of the team. It's important firstly that you have them behind you in the difficult period to come and secondly that you can weigh up the strengths and weaknesses of your case. Another viewpoint, perhaps with someone acting as Devil's Advocate, could help clarify your position.

Let me warn you off protests against decisions of Judges of Fact. If you've been caught in illegal servicing, if you've been adjudged to have jumped a stage start or if you've taken a wrong route on a stage, then my advice, unless you have strong, independent evidence to refute the claim, would be to forget it; swallow your pride, accept your fate and put the episode down to experience. Always make sure of your legal ground before proceeding. Check out the Blue Book, though this may sometimes appear to offer conflicting solutions. Finally, make sure you understand the procedures for protests laid out therein.

If you must go ahead with your protest, then you should make it within the specified time period, as laid down in the regulations. There have been occasions when competitors have turned up late to check the results, only to find that they've already gone final and the time for protests has passed. In this case you forfeit your ability to protest, so always go and check the results just in case some timing or computation anomaly has crept in unnoticed. When making your protest, you should submit in writing an outline of your grounds for the claim, together with the requisite fee. At a specified time, the stewards will convene and may ask you to present your claim more fully. It's best if one of you, usually the co-driver, acts as the spokesman. You may call other people—competitors, marshals, etc.—to give evidence. The organizers, or other affected competitors, may also give evidence against your case. Once again, keep calm and lucid. After the hearing, the stewards will consider the case 'in camera'. Later they may call you back in to announce their verdict (and whether the fee is returnable) and then publish the outcome by bulletin. If it affects the results, the organizers must now amend these and declare them provisional again, to allow others affected by the changes to make their protest within the allotted period. All rather messy and best avoided if you can.

If you're not happy with the result of the protest hearing and you're sure that you do have strong grounds for taking things further, you are allowed to appeal to the RAC MSA. But we're now talking serious legal disputes here, so you should be convinced of your case before taking this drastic step. Even though you may feel you've been badly treated, consider if it's really worth going to these lengths to get satisfaction. We are talking about a sport here. Perhaps in the heat of the moment you may feel you must go on as a matter of principle, but in my view there are rarely any 'winners' in this situation; only the sport suffers from protracted wranglings, and whatever the outcome, the victorious party rarely comes out with any credit.

It may be that you yourself are the subject of a protest by another competitor, or that the organizers request the stewards to impose some penalty on you at their discretion, such as for a traffic violation. You can still present your case as above, but remember to be straightforward and courteous, even if things go against you. Losing your temper may well lose you the benefit of the doubt as well as bring about possible further penalties. Let's hope it rarely, if ever, comes to such a situation for you. Protests and appeals are not pleasant situations and are best avoided wherever possible. Remember, at the end of the day, it's a sport.

So, let's get away from the rather negative aspect of problems and look at an area where a co-driver can make a more positive contribution.

Part 3

CULTURED
CO-DRIVING

Chapter 11

Pace notes

The basis of British club rallying is the 'blind' format, whether on forestry or other surfaces, so you shouldn't have the need for pace notes in the early events of your career. In mainland Britain, partly because we cannot as yet have public road closures for rallying, you will only encounter pace notes at International level, as pioneered by the Scottish or RAC Rallies, though the situation may well change as other events follow suit. In the Isle of Man and Ireland, however, closed public roads are available, so some National and most International events there can be done on pace notes. If you venture further afield, to almost any part of Europe, you will find that pace notes are the norm, at all levels. So let's see what they're all about.

Pace notes are basically a description of the road ahead. When read out correctly, they give the driver an accurate assessment of the speed at which he can take the next stretch of road. Particularly when the view of the road is poor, because of high banks or walls, or blind crests, or in poor visibility weather conditions, pace notes make the task of driving safer, because hidden hazards are (or should be) annotated. They also make it faster, because corners which appear tighter than they really are can be taken much quicker than they would be in a 'blind' situation.

As the notes are read out by the co-driver, quite a few people believe that they are actually made by him. This is rarely the case, though in 1982 Walter Rohrl won the Ivory Coast Rally entirely on notes made by his co-driver Christian Geistdorfer, since he himself was reluctant to recce this rather strange event. Under normal circumstances, the co-driver writes down the driver's assessment of the road and on the event delivers the same words back to him, timed to come out a little before the driver reaches the corner, hazard or straight so described.

This is not quite as easy as it sounds, and particularly with an inexperienced crew mishaps are possible, either through an error in the notes (in the rating or the reading), over-confidence in the notes, or the driver not listening to the notes. Some perseverance will be required to correct these problems.

There are several systems in use and though there may be similarities in each driver's method of assessing the road, the end result will be individual to that particular driver. One driver, used to a particular system, could live with the notes of another driver on the same system, but would not be totally confident in them. Assessments of straights, corners, lines and hazards are highly subjective and no two drivers see things, and hence describe things, in exactly the same way. To be honest, it really doesn't matter how you describe a succession of corners. It could be 'pink left into blue right' or 'Donald Duck left and Mickey Mouse right' (I haven't actually done a rally with a driver who does it in these ways), it makes no difference, so long—and it's a big proviso—so long as the driver understands instantly and precisely what those terms mean. What is not always appreciated is that the co-driver must also understand the significance of the descriptions, otherwise to him he's reading out a load of nonsense and cannot relate it to the road ahead, in which case he will lose his place and the notes will be ineffective, if not dangerous. So both crew members have to understand the system instantaneously; there's no time for thinking about it.

On the continent, in areas where crews have become used to high-speed recceing, the more common systems seem to be ones based either on the actual speed of the corner or on the correct gear for the corner, expressed in numbers and/or words. Personally, I have my reservations about this method, because surely in weather conditions different from practice these descriptions must be incorrect. Nevertheless they seem to work (I assume the drivers have some mental downgrading or upgrading process which compensates for this situation)— witness the number of highly successful southern European crews around at present, many of whom use these methods. I did some rallies with Harald Demuth, a top German driver, who had a system loosely linked to the appropriate gear, i.e. '1' was a very tight first gear corner and '6' was a very fast top gear corner. Shortly after this I started rallying with David Llewellin, who also uses a number system, but for him '1' is fast and '6' is very slow, which I found very confusing at first, after what I'd got used to with Harald.

The number system does seem to be gaining in acceptance, because it's simple, logical and easy to read out. Numbers are short words and are not abbreviations, so they're instantly readable. If six numbers isn't enough for you, you can always add more as you develop your pace note method. For someone starting out rallying, I would suggest that they begin with a number system from scratch, because what you learn in those early formative events tends to stick with you for ever. David Llewellin began with a number system simply because for an early rally he borrowed a set of car preparer Phil Collins's notes which happened to use this method. Of course people can change their system later, but it wastes valuable on-event time as they adapt to their new ways.

Finally, there's the descriptive system, which many drivers in

Below *David Llewellin's pace notes, showing his use of the number system.* (Lodge.)

Bottom *Malcolm Wilson's pace notes for the same piece of stage, using the descriptive system.* (Lodge.)

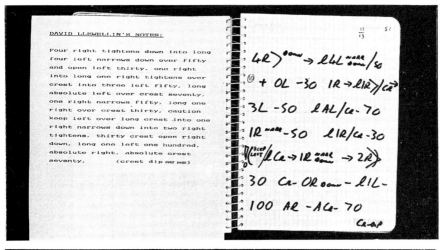

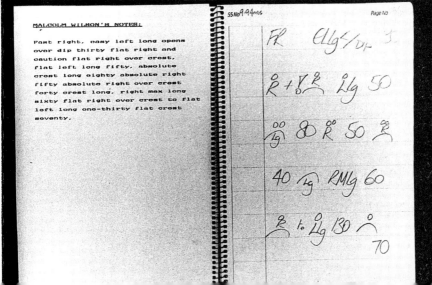

the UK seem to use. This stems from the fact that basically we invented pace notes in the first place and secondly that short Anglo-Saxon words lend themselves to this type of work. 'Flat', 'fast', 'open', 'sharp', 'hard', 'easy', 'bad', 'tight', 'square' are all words which trip readily off the tongue. Their French, Italian, German or Scandinavian equivalents generally contain more syllables and are therefore harder to say in a hurry. However, for the sake of compactness in the writing, you will probably have to abbreviate the words to the initial one or two letters and get used to unscrambling them instantly and without thought. Even a descriptive system will use numbers for distances, while a number system will also use descriptions for some aspects, such as a crest, a tightening bend or a jump, so perhaps it's erroneous to categorize these methods as entirely different. For comparison, see the page of Malcolm Wilson's notes (descriptive) and of David Llewellin's notes (numbers) for the same piece of road.

First notes

For your first rally on pace notes, it would make a lot of sense to make use of someone else's notes. Quite often there are commercially available notes for these events, but you should try to get notes made to a system that your driver would like to adopt. Ask around until you find what you're looking for. This may mean photocopying another competitor's notes or borrowing his last year's notes, but at least it will get you going, so that you can see how notes are made. Your driver may not entirely like them, but you can modify them as you check the stages. Then he's on his way to developing his own system. You may already have some sort of method established from reading off the map in the forests, but beware: the map reading is a purely geographical or 'static' system, geared to what the map tells you. Pace notes should be more of a 'dynamic' system, geared to what the rally car is expected to be doing, speed- or attitude-wise. For this very reason, David Llewellin and I had different systems for 'blind' forest and for pace notes.

Where only low-speed recceing is allowed (as in the UK), the driver needs to develop the skill of assessing what the rally car is going to do at speed. Quite often we would find that the notes didn't flow too well at recce speeds, but on the event they would work really well; that's the sign of a good set of notes. It's rather like a fighter aircraft: at low speeds it's very difficult to fly, but at high speeds it really comes into its own.

Refining the system

While it may seem easy to pick up someone else's notes and go rallying, it's not really the ideal, because as you both develop stronger opinions on how notes should be made and written, you will spend increasingly more time amending the other person's notes and thereby waste valuable recce time, possibly losing the 'flow' of the notes in the process if you're having to stop and start all the time. So you and your driver should look to start making your own at the earliest opportunity. Once you've got the general basis of your system established, I would sugggest you both go out into the local countryside one day and practise making your own on a selection of roads. Obviously you can't check them at rally speed, but at least you'll get some idea of how they work out.

Undoubtedly on your first read-back, the driver will find that some of his assessments are wrong. The most common fault is mistaking the distances, but some of the corners too will be wrong, particularly when in a close succession to one another. To resolve the former, the driver needs to practise estimating distances every time he goes out driving on normal roads. If he can temporarily fit a trip meter in his car he can check his assessments until accuracy becomes second nature. There's nothing worse than inconsistent, 'elastic' distances in the pace notes.

Accuracy of corner assessment comes only with experience, as does the ability to group together a sequence of corners. If you have two or three fast corners followed by a tight one, then the whole sequence must be read out together, otherwise on the rally you'll arrive at the bad corner too quickly or on the wrong line. Not recommended. Get the driver to say where he wants a series of corners read out together, though be careful not to include too much as he will be 'overloaded'. Some co-drivers underline the corners to be linked, but if in the future, perhaps on an Irish or foreign rally, you have the benefit of a 'gravel crew' or 'ice note crew' (see Chapter 12), the information from these people tends to be in the form of underlining, which then clashes with your own underlining. So my suggestion is that you bracket the linked corners, leaving the underside clear for other markings.

If a junction comes along, I suggest you use, depending on its shape, the words 'turn' or 'tee' or 'straight' (in the case of going over a cross-roads) as the type of junction warrants. The driver may not need to know that it's a junction, but it certainly will be useful to you, to check your place and in case you use parts of the same stage in the future, in which case it's simpler to find the right bit of road. Learn to use the words 'long', 'tightens', 'opens' and 'narrows' for non-standard corners which incorporate those traits. Linking corners together with 'and' and 'into' is useful where there is no significant distance between them, though be careful to get your distinction between the two correct. I use a '—' where there is no distance, with the next instruction immediate, and I use the same symbol to hang the next distance onto a corner, as the driver usually likes to know this so that he can get the power on that little bit earlier. However, these are just my ideas—I don't want to influence you too much, as the making and the writing of the notes should be things personal to your driver and you. You can make them how you want.

Try to be sparing with 'cautions'—for something tricky or deceptive—and 'dangers'—where there is something really dangerous. Over-use will simply devalue them to the point that when you have something really bad, you won't fully appreciate it until too late. Changes in surface need to be marked down, for instance going from tarmac to gravel or vice versa, as do places where water collects and, if on tarmac, sections where the tar changes to that very shiny variety, because in the wet this is like ice to drive on. Stones on the edges of corners need attention. One year on the Circuit of Ireland we picked up a puncture during the recce. I was a bit miffed at the time, as it wasted valuable recce period, but when we checked why, it was a really jagged rock, well hidden in the grass. We marked it in the notes and on the rally had no problems, but the carnage that rock was to cause with the rest of the field on the event had to be seen to be believed. Any sort of obstruction on the inside of the corner should be annotated with the words 'Don't cut' or similar, as these cover a multitude of sins and are quick and easy to say along with the corner description.

Encourage your driver to think in terms of what the rally car will be doing, rather than the actual geography of the road, not just for the corners but also the straights, downhills, bumps, jumps and dips. On the Ulster Rally one year we got caught out by a set of small ripples in the road which were virtually imperceptible at 40 mph in a standard Montego, but at 120 mph in a Metro 6R4 were highly dangerous. These launched us off the road and out of the event. These are the sort of things your driver must be looking for and again experience, sometimes of the bitter kind, will tell. However, the overriding principle on which the notes are made should be 'simplicity'. Don't let your driver put masses of detail in, as neither of you is going to be able to cope with it all, especially at speed. Keep it

Right *'Don't cut' is a good instruction to apply to any place where the driver might find problems if tempted to drive over the apex. (Lodge.)*

Below *A piece of board, 18in x 12in, makes a good base for writing the pace notes in the car.*

Below right *With road book and pace note book clipped to the board, you can keep your place and get the notes down on paper.*

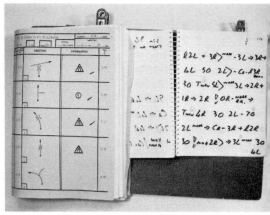

short and simple; you can always add 'tweaks' later, but it's very difficult actually to remove something from the system and bad habits acquired now will lead to trouble in future.

Another point to look out for is places where the visibility line deceives the eye, such as a firebreak or a line of telegraph poles. On the recce the driver may not notice the danger, because he's concentrating so much on the road and making notes. At speed on the rally, especially if he's not concentrating fully on the notes, he could be deceived into going off the road. Try to spot such places yourself during the recce and mention them to the driver. He can then decide whether to add a caution or some other comment that will draw his attention during the event.

Writing down

Good or bad, you still have to get the pace notes down on paper. Firstly, you need a firm base. I had a piece of board, 18in by 12in, which I found ideal for clipping the road book to the left side and the pace note book to the right, though I suppose if you're left-handed it would work the other way round. You need to have the road book to hand, open at the right page to keep your place and navigate the driver on the right road. It is not much use making notes of the wrong bit of road. Your pace note book should be a reasonably sized spiral-bound notebook. There are purpose-made books available commercially, though these are not cheap, but you can use the type found in most stationers. The only problem with these, I find, is that the spiral is rather too small, making the pages harder to turn in a hurry and therefore leading to snagging and tearing under the stress of rapid page-turning.

There are two schools of thought about the writing. You can write them down in rough and then copy them out neatly later, or you can go for the main 'write' at the first attempt. The advantage of the former is that you can create a neater final appearance and eradicate errors/corrections in the re-writing stage; you will also make the notes a little quicker. The disadvantage is that this involves you in a lot of rewriting work. If time is tight, you'll find yourself doing this work into the small hours of the morning and quite probably making errors in the copying out. If your next run is during the rally, that will be disastrous.

The advantage of writing the actual notes at the time is that 'what you see is what you get', so the making of errors or missing something out is all but eliminated. The correction of errors is taken care of by some (hopefully) minor tidying-up work in the evening, allowing you to relax more, ready for the next day's activities. The disadvantage is that the final presentation is not quite so tidy, especially with the amendments, and if, like me, your handwriting is not of the neatest quality, it's quite hard on the recce to write legibly, especially on bumpy roads or gravel surfaces. For this reason, if on this

Pace note books are commercially available, but you can use normal spiral-bound books from a stationery shop.

method, you must ask the driver to drive a little slower in the 'making' phase. Personally. I prefer it this way anyway.

If writing in rough it doesn't really matter what you use to write the initial notes. If writing for real you can either write in pencil or pen. Don't write too close to the edge of the page (you have to put your hands somewhere), nor try to cram too much onto a page (there should be plenty of pages). I find that pencil is not always easy to read, especially under the map light, while ball point pen is rather too fine. I use a medium nib permanent felt tip pen: medium nib to give a bold appearance, easy to read in all lighting conditions; permanent so it doesn't run if wet through rain or sweaty palms. What about corrections? On the check run I make the corrections in pencil, then in my tidying up session at the end of the day I use typist's correcting fluid and when this is dry I write with felt tip over the top. However, each co-driver tends to develop his own preferences in this aspect, so it's really up to you to find the way that suits you best.

Other tweaks I do in my tidying up session: put the cautions/dangers in red felt tip (this draws my attention to them as I approach them in the rally); put the first instruction from the next page in the bottom right corner of the previous page (this is to guard against turning over two pages at once); add the overall page numbers as well as the page numbers per stage (the former to provide an index, allowing you to find your way to the relevant notes easily; the latter to tell you how many pages to go to the stage finish, a rough distance guide). It's also useful to put at the start of the stage the stage distance, a description of the surface(s) and a few words outlining the nature of the stage, together with a tyre recommendation. This will help the driver's memory when you come back on the rally, as will comments such as 'This is where we met the dustcart round the bad right-hander'. Note down the exact place where the notes start; next year the start could be slightly different and you'll wonder why you can't get the notes to match up. Also, continue the notes some way after the (marked) flying finish, as you'll still be at speed for some distance before the stop board. Finally, add the junction numbers for the same reason as I suggested you add them to your forestry maps, i.e. for rapid identification of trouble spots.

Organizing the recce

Once again, we're back to that word organization. Obviously, it depends on the type of recce you're allowed, but you should seek to extract as much out of the recce period as you possibly

A trip-meter in the recce car is useful, not only for finding the way, but also for the driver to check his distances accurately. This car, used by the author and David Llewellin for the 1990 RAC recce, has one trip-meter for the driver and one for the co-driver. (Hodson/CCC.)

can. Here in the UK we tend to have restricted practice periods in standard cars. On the continent, recceing is freer with regard to the time period and the car, though public opinion is now forcing some constraints on those practices. For British events, you will need a standard car according to the recce regulations, preferably close to the type of car you will use on the rally. If your rally car is left hand drive, so should your recce car be, as the driver's view is slightly different from the other side of the car. A trip meter would help enormously, so that you don't waste valuable time exploring the wrong roads, especially in Ireland where there are many small roads leading off the route. Take a look at where you should be and when, if it's a convoy-type recce, so that you don't miss your 'slot'. You may have to 'register' for the recce, either at the beginning or even daily. This is so that the organizers can keep tabs on you and issue the relevant admonishments if necessary.

If recceing is limited to certain hours, try to get your travelling to and from the stages done outside these hours, so that you can maximize the time available actually on the stages. In making my plan for the recce, I try to guess the obvious point where the majority will start (e.g. Stage 1) and then go somewhere completely different. This generally ensures that the stages are freer of others recceing (and of organizer's checks), so note making is easier, without interruptions caused by the car in front stopping and starting. A driver needs a clear view of the road ahead to make and check his notes; other note-making cars are therefore a distraction, as well as a temptation to stop and chat, thus wasting valuable recce period. In time, experience will tell you what you can achieve in a day's recceing, but make a plan, perhaps a slightly optimistic plan to cover you if things go really well, and tick off the stages as you 'make' and 'check', so you don't miss anything out.

You will be restricted to certain speeds on the stages, so you should encourage your driver to stick to these if you are to avoid upsetting the locals or incurring penalties from the organizers. Remember too that you will probably be recceing in a rural community, where the roads are normally very quiet, with the locals not expecting someone driving along 'their' bit of road. Don't expect the roads to be entirely free—quite often you will meet large, lumbering farm vehicles. Standards of local driving and speed of reactions may not be on a par with your own. Expect the unexpected and you should stay out of trouble. If your driver takes chances with speed or commitment, sooner or later he will have an accident, which will cost you a large amount of valuable recce time, as well as any other consequences of the crash. Think too about the rally's relations with the locals. If we upset too many people, we will lose stages and ultimately rallies as well.

Of course, you can press ahead on the link sections in between the stages to maintain your schedule. Some people never stop for lunch during the recce, but I think it's a good idea to get out of the car for a while, to have a stretch and a bit of refreshment. That way, you won't get as bored and fed up with practice, while with a bit of grub inside you, you won't run out of steam later on in the afternoon and lose concentration. If your lunch break is likely to be somewhere away from civilization, you can always take a packed lunch and drinks with you. Recceing is hard work for both of you, but that's not to say it can't be fun. A good recce can set you up for a really good event; a poor recce will leave you not entirely confident with the notes you have made and not too positive about the event itself.

Limited recce

A few events, like the current Scottish Rally, allow just one run over the stages. This will demand the utmost concentration from both of you, as you have no chance to check for errors. Though I've enjoyed the Scottish—and that includes the recces—I'm not convinced that this is the best way. There have been driving errors which surely arose from unchecked notes, while there is quite an advantage to having notes from the previous year, which penalizes newcomers. The convoy system also works against good, clear note-making; following other cars in a slow-moving queue makes it very hard to concentrate on things like distances and bumps. Try to get your driver to hang back so that he gets a clear view of the road. The main thing is for both of you to concentrate really hard, so that you get it as right as possible.

The RAC Rally presently allows two runs over the stages, which is certainly more than twice as good as one run. I have personal views about the decision to allow recceing at all on the RAC, as this has robbed World Championship rallying of one of the great driving and co-driving challenges, but I'll not bore you with all the ramifications of that. Again, you need a lot of concentration and you may not get the notes quite perfect, but at least they should be more or less correct. The schedule is fairly tight as you have to pack in quite a lot of stages (twice) in each day, as well as a lot more road mileage than usual, so again it's especially important that you are in the right place at the right time and don't find any trouble that will delay you substantially. You won't get a second chance to get on the stages that you miss.

On events like the Ulster Rally you have a limited number of days to complete your recce, so you can do the stages in any order and as many times as the hours permit. Generally, over four days I found it was possible to do every stage three times comfortably, four times if all went well. So my plan would be to 'make', 'check' and 'check'—this gets the notes pretty well correct—and then on the final day go for one run through the lot. This means that the driver is taking a fresh look at the stages (and may pick up the odd mistake) on the final run and is forced really to listen to the notes, rather than relying on memory as he would if we went for three 'checks' on the initial run. He also gets to see each stage on the last day before the rally, which is good for his confidence.

Manx recce

The Manx International Rally is closer to the European norm, in that once the road book is published (a few weeks before the event), crews are free to recce when they wish. They can even recce at night-time. The Isle of Man is a pretty small place and realistically you can 'make', then 'check' three times comfortably over a long weekend, even with certain restrictions of the times for using the stages because of two-directional use. I would recommend that you don't do this just before the rally, as by then the roads are full of everybody recceing or checking their notes, not to mention holidaymakers and motorbike enthusiasts; try to go there fairly early to make and check your notes while things are quiet, then return for the rally and have a final couple of runs just to see that all is well.

In fact, what happens on the Manx is that quite a few drivers know the stages so well that the notes are almost, but not totally, superfluous. To do this they need to spend a lot of time on the island, even without the co-driver, just memorizing the relatively few roads. After David Llewellin and I had made and checked the notes, I used to send him out on his own for exactly this purpose. Another little 'tweak' of the Manx, though it applies to some other rallies as well, is to 'trip' all the distances on high ground accurately. This is because low cloud can affect the island, and with the distances 'tripped', you can count down the straights even in thick fog and therefore be much quicker. It has to be absolutely right though.

Overseas recce

Overseas events are generally run on similar lines for recceing as the Manx, with practice being relatively free. So while you're not under so much time pressure, you do need to see that your recce is effective as you will be up against locals who know their way around pretty well. There are some limited recce rallies, like the Hunsrück Rally in Germany, which has a convoy system with two runs over the stages, but this is an exception brought about by its use of the military ranges on which the event is based. Rallies in Belgium tend to consist of two or three laps of the same stages, so recceing is much easier than, say, in Ireland. Though there are signs of increasing restriction on high speed practice, a few events still allow you to recce in full-blown rally cars, especially where the roads are rough and tough, but we're talking very serious expenditure now and really only for the works or big-sponsor teams on World or European Championship rallies.

Hire cars

If you don't take your own recce car, then be careful if you hire a car for this purpose. Many hire companies are 'wise' to the rally recce and specifically (and understandably) prohibit use of their cars for this purpose. You may therefore be driving without insurance and will certainly be expected to pay for all damages, including tyre wear and underbody damage, resulting from recce use. In my experience, hire cars make poor recce cars in any case, as their lights, tyres, brakes and suspension are rarely up to the required standard and they're

not equipped for the job (no map light or trip-meter, for instance), so this is not the ideal solution.

Reading the notes

Your pre-event familiarization and the recce should have shown you how to read the notes but of course things will happen much more quickly on the event itself. To some extent, you're in the hands of your driver, in more ways than one. If he has given you some very complex and detailed notes, then maybe you're going to struggle to get the information out. Just as important, the driver is going to struggle to understand it. So, as we said earlier, the objective should be to keep it straightforward and simple. If you have problems in this area, you must discuss it with the driver, so that he simplifies his information next time. Don't just let the situation worsen. Even Luis Moya had to get World Champion Carlos Sainz to trim down his notes during their first championship winning season, so it happens to the best.

Timing

As you read the notes on a stage, you need to develop a timing that delivers them at just the right moment, not too soon—or the driver will forget what you've said—nor too late—as you'll probably end up off the road. Not everyone can achieve that timing, especially on their early events, but with perseverance (and some tolerance from the driver) it should come right. To get the timing right, you need to be referring both to the notes and to the road. If you look up, there's a risk of losing your place, so either learn to come back to exactly the right place every time or keep your finger near the last instruction read out. You can feel by the movement of the car where you are in the notes, but you will still have to glance up every so often to confirm your position, otherwise the timing will be out. Don't gabble and don't shout, but do put some expression into it. David Llewellin reckoned he knew almost as much from the tone of my voice as from the words as to what was about to come up next.

As you approach the page turn-over point, run one finger under the page you're reading, ready to flip it over, checking you don't turn over two pages. (The over-page note in the bottom right hand corner should help prevent this, or at least help you to spot the error before you read out a wrong note.) Sod's Law will determine that your driver quite often puts in something tricky right after turn-over point. If something distracts you, like the driver having a slight off or near miss, or asking you to switch something on, or some sort of car problem, it's very easy to lose your place—and surprisingly hard to pick it up again. If this happens, tell the driver he's on his own and try to find where you are on the notes. Usually, you can do this within a few corners. If the driver mishears you, he should say 'repeat', so you can read the last group of notes to him again. If the driver feels there is an incipient car problem, he may ask you how long to go, in which case the stage page numbers should tell you without you having to take your eyes

Above left *'Change that note to a "flat"'—Malcolm Wilson tweaks up his notes prior to winning the 1990 Mobil Challenge. (Not so sure about the clothing, lads.)* (Kolczak.)

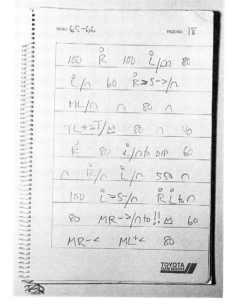

Right *Sometimes, when a road section is tight, you need to pace note it. Bjorn Waldegaard/Fred Gallagher, Safari Rally, 1990.*

189

off the page to look at the trip-meter. I found that generally we got about one mile for every pace note page, though on very twisty stages, this would come down to about 1 km or 0.6 mile. Finally, if you go off as a result of an incorrect pace note, make sure you have a pencil ready to make the necessary, but belated, correction, though that may be the least of your problems at the time.

Don't worry if the pace notes don't work too well to begin with. At times the driver will be underconfident and therefore slower than without notes; at other times, he'll feel the notes are working so well, he'll become overconfident and go off. If you're both starting from scratch it'll take at least a season to get things really sorted so that you both fully trust each other. And that's the whole basis, really, one of trust and team effort. When you've got the system refined, the timing's spot on and you're working well, there's a tremendous feeling of satisfaction for the co-driver. After all, you're contributing almost as much to the speed as the driver himself. In a way, what you're doing with the book and the words equates to what the driver is doing with the car and the road. When he commits flat out over a blind brow, and it's right, you'll know you're doing a good job on the notes.

Chapter 12

Going overseas

Your initial experience of crossing water from the UK to go rallying may well be for rallies in the Isle of Man or Ireland. Good rallies they are too, from the aspect of experience and seeing the sport in a different light, possibly through the bottom of a Guinness glass. Rallying in Ireland is a very enjoyable experience, in a relaxed kind of way. The people are very friendly, very enthusiastic and while some things are not always done according to the book, no-one seems to mind too much. So it's really not too difficult to go rallying there. Quite a few of the lesser events are open to non-homologated cars, so you should have no excuse for not giving Irish rallying a try. You'll enjoy it. For some events you'll need to do a recce, as we've already covered in the previous chapter, and your tyres will primarily need to be racing type for the bumpy tarmac lanes. Otherwise, it's not too different in co-driving terms from rallying on the mainland.

Foreign events

Though that small strip of water across to the continent is much smaller than the Irish Sea, many British rally teams are for some reason reluctant to venture across it for their sport. Perhaps the Channel Tunnel will alter this, but maybe a change in attitude is also needed. Basically, we tend to be wrapped up in our domestic championships, leaving little in the way of ambition or budget for going abroad. However, the idea that all rallies on the continent are expensive is a myth. The World Championship rallies can be very expensive (though some British privateers have contrived to do Sweden or 1000 Lakes on spectacularly low budgets), but there are many rallies in France and Belgium which are easy to do, enjoyable and give you good experience. Quite often the organizers will

Belgian events are easy to do and enjoyable, with plenty of media and spectator interest. (Kolczak.)

do a 'deal' specifically to attract foreign privateers, which might include ferry concessions, free or very cheap hotels, free entry and service plates, free petrol and even start money or local sponsorship. Now you're not going to pick up all of those benefits, particularly if you're a complete unknown in an unfancied car, but you should get some of the concessions even so. If you do your sums, you may well come to the conclusion that it costs no more—it may even cost less—than doing an International in the UK.

Event organisers

As co-driver, it will probably fall to your lot to make enquiries about a foreign venture. You can find out about foreign rallies

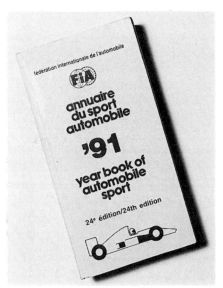

Left *The 'Yellow Book'—the FIA Year Book. Essential for International rallying.*

Right *You will need a homologated car and the homologation papers to prove it. (Lodge.)*

Far right *Check the tyre regulations—some countries (UK included) demand grooving, others allow pure slicks. (Kolczak.)*

offering such deals in the motor sporting magazines, but if you know a competitor who has been abroad, ask him about a good event to go for. You will need to get yourself a 'Yellow Book', which is the *FIA Yearbook of Automobile Sport*. FISA (Federation Internationale du Sport Automobile) is the sporting arm of the FIA (Fédération Internationale de l'Automobile) and administers the sport at International level. You will be encouraged to know that all FIA-sanctioned events are run to a standard set of regulations, as are UK Internationals, so you should have few problems with the rules or format, apart from one or two local variations. To find the organizers, look them up in the 'Yellow Book', which lists each FIA-approved event and then its organizers by number code. Write to them explaining your interest and ask for the concessions they are prepared to offer—you could be agreeably surprised by the response.

The car

Assuming your driver is similarly enthusiastic, then you need to set things in motion, much as you would for a UK event. There are some additional requirements, however. Rallying on the continent is done almost entirely according to FISA vehicle regulations, so if you haven't got access to a homologated car, you might have to go further than just across the channel— Spain for example—to do your foreign rally. My first foreign rally was actually in Romania (with bits of Austria and Hungary thrown in) and there's even less obstacle now to going into

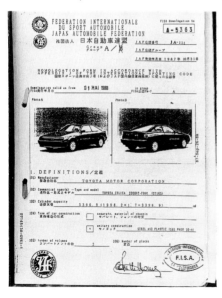

Eastern Europe for rallying. However, let's assume that you have a homologated car (and the homologation papers to prove it). You need to check the tyre regulations, regarding racing tyres and studded tyres, where applicable. Some countries allow full, ungrooved slicks; others, like Belgium, have their own rules on grooving and on studded tyres, so make sure you can comply before setting off. The tyre grooving rules may not be the same as you've encountered in the UK and Ireland.

Visa

There was a time when you had to arrange a separate visa each time you wished to compete abroad. Basically the RAC MSA needed to assure itself that you (the driver, the co-driver and the entrant) were of sufficient standard to compete abroad and were covered by at least some basic insurance in case of accident. However, this involved additional administration for everyone concerned. Thankfully, the RAC MSA now includes the visa on your International Licence, on the basis that if you've gone through the process of qualifying for the licence, you should be capable of competing satisfactorily at that level. The only point to remember is to make sure that the event organizers realize that the visa is part of your licence, as they may be expecting a separate visa under the old system. Perhaps if you attach a photocopy of your competition licence(s) with your entry form, this will solve the problem.

Insurance

Insurance is another aspect: insurance for the rally car—normally a green card will suffice, though you should check that this will cover you for use on the rally; insurance for your service vehicle(s) and parts/equipment; insurance for yourselves and the service crew. It's surprising what can go wrong when you go abroad, so some sort of accident and medical cover would be wise, though the standard travel policy usually excludes coverage for competitive sports. You may have to contact the specialists listed in the Blue Book. You will almost certainly be required to produce the rally car's registration document at scrutineering, so make sure that goes along too, as well as your usual selection of licences and other documents. May I insult your intelligence by also reminding you to ensure that everyone takes their passport? Dover is not a good place to discover that somebody's passport is missing.

Customs

While this may be the era of the European Community, don't feel that you can set off to cross borders without any paperwork. So often, an inexperienced team comes unstuck on its first trip overseas through having little or no customs documentation. What you need, at the time of writing, is something called an ATA Carnet and you can get details of these at your local Chamber of Commerce. Basically, a Carnet is a guarantee that the parts and equipment you bring into a country will be taken out again within a certain period. So, equipped with the Carnet, you won't have to pay import duty or VAT on your bits and pieces. Without it, a customs official is quite within his rights to ask you (or your service crew) to pay these sums before proceeding.

The Carnet contains several duplicate pages listing all the parts on board, including wheels and tyres and as you leave the UK, the British customs will remove one page and stamp the counterfoil. On arrival at the, say, French customs they will do the same and then when you return, repeat the process. They may well check your load to see that you are not now returning with an empty van and in any case they will check their records to see that the paperwork matches up. This can take time. What you must avoid, at all costs, is to fail to go through this procedure at any border. Remember, crossing from, say, Belgium to Germany will involve one leaving visit to the Belgian customs and one arriving visit to the German customs for the Carnet routine. If you omit just one process, then technically you have failed to export/import your parts and the bond, which someone will have to put up on the Carnet in the first place, will be forfeit. The whole process is repeated on your return journey, including coming back into the UK. In your scheduling, you should allow an extra hour at each border post to cover these formalities. It can take less; at busy crossings, where you're jockeying for position with dozens of burly truck drivers, also armed with Carnets, it can take much longer.

One final word: don't be tempted to sell or dispose of parts which are on your Carnet. Some motor sporting outfits have brought rallying a bad name for this or other irregularities in the past. It's just not worth the substantial penalties involved.

Other arrangements

The hotel may well be provided by the organizers as part of your 'deal'. It may be free or at least very cheap; when you arrive there you may, if unlucky, realize why. But it's all part of the adventure and if there's a gang of you (quite often they'll put all the Brits into one establishment), you'll soon forget the bed bugs, draughty windows and raucous traffic noise as you set about enjoying the experience of rallying abroad. If you have to book the hotel yourself, then usually the local tourist office will help, or you can delve into one of the hotel guides, like *Michelin*, for inspiration. If you make your plans late, you can expect to be staying quite some distance away from the rally centre.

The ferry should be quite straightforward to organize, though remember that the boat will not wait for your van if it's stuck in customs, so do make sufficient allowance for such delays. Depending on the size of your vehicle(s), some countries have restrictions on the driving of them at weekends, while the French police, I'm told, do take a delight in stopping people for speeding; the fines are heavy and on the spot. Some countries, like France and Italy, have motorway tolls, which can mount up considerably on a long trek, so include that in your budgeting. You can get guidance on all these matters from your local AA travel office.

The recce

As we've already covered most aspects of this activity, let's just look at the differences. First of all, the style of recce is a lot more free, generally, than in the UK. Normally you are allowed to recce from when the road book is issued. In some cases that could be a month before the rally. For a big World Championship event, you could need most of that period, but for the average European rally a few days is normally quite sufficient. In Belgium, the rally format is generally laps of the same, or similar, stages, so the actual mileage you need to note is often quite small. If sections of stages are common, rather than a complete stage, then you can either write each stage separately, or arrange your notes so that you can turn to the link section and back again. It must be foolproof on the event though—no good turning to the wrong page. To aid myself in this situation, I would use one or more of those extra big paper clips to keep the correct page ready.

Although the regulations on recceing are becoming stricter, in some parts of Europe practice is regarded by the spectators as part of the entertainment, so they will come to watch in the anticipation of some excitement. The pace of recceing may well be quicker than you're allowed at home. When practising in Italy one year, Malcolm Wilson and I were staggered to be

Where you need to link multi use sections of the pace notes, use a large paper clip to keep the place.

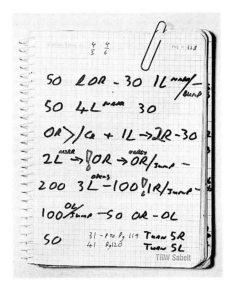

overtaken by an Autobianchi A112, of all things, going flat out on a twisty downhill section in broad daylight. If you're going to emulate the locals in this form of recce, then first of all you need a reasonably prepared recce car, with decent tyres, suspension, brakes and lights. A completely standard car just won't last long at that sort of pace—hence my advice not to use a hire car for recces.

Once you've made the notes and checked them for basic accuracy by day, you are generally permitted to recce at night time. This means you can go quicker, to test the speed-accuracy of the notes, because usually—but not always—you can spot the headlights of anything coming the other way. However, let me issue a note of caution. This form of recceing can be very anti-social. Each local resident disturbed, each bit of property damaged, each family pet or farm animal maimed or killed or each innocent local involved in a road accident, is yet another nail in rallying's coffin in that particular area. So I would urge you and your driver to be as responsible as possible if indulging in a high-speed recce. The future of rallying is in your hands.

The event

Many foreign events make much more promotional mileage (or is that kilometrage?) out of documentation and scrutineering. So that these things can be stage-managed, you may well have to clock in at a specific time at scrutineering, as at a normal time control. If yours is a turbo car, there will probably be a

separate turbo scrutineering session earlier, at which you must present the car and all your spare turbos for sealing of the restrictors. You may also have to present your overalls to show that they possess the FISA homologation mark. Documentation is much the same as at home.

The start will feature even more of the razzamatazz. Events like the 24 Hours of Ypres have a very professional set up, with the start ramp in the town square, surrounded by hospitality units for the sponsors and just about every available space covered by advertising hoardings. The atmosphere is electric and the crowds enormous, even before you get to the stages. The police tend to keep the roads clearer than they do on UK rallies and generally give rally cars the sort of priority that cycle racers expect on the continent. The traffic on the roads will generally tolerate a rally car coming past them to make a time control on time. Service time on the lesser events tends to be none too generous out on the road sections and road penalties vary from five seconds per minute late to one minute per minute—quite tough.

Service rules are more relaxed. In many countries you can service almost anywhere, even at the roadside after every stage. The road book will contain some indication as to whether this is allowed on a particular section or not. In some parts of the world, the only restriction may be that the service point must be off the public road or on private property. You can expect a centralized service location at the end of a lap—usually in a town square, accompanied by still more atmosphere! All this unaccustomed service may stretch your support facilities. If limited in terms of vehicle numbers, then you need to select the important places for service and maybe go two or three stages without assistance in a few areas. You might be able to fill these gaps with a chase car, or perhaps by sharing service with a similarly seeded fellow Brit with a similar car. However, these plans may go out of the window after the halt, if the two cars are reseeded a long way apart.

Time control

I generally find overseas marshals and officials much more knowledgeable on the rules and regulations than their British counterparts. That's not to knock the British officials, who are usually a friendly, capable bunch, but in the past they have perhaps been unaware of the FISA way of doing things or have been poorly briefed by the chief marshal or preferred to do

Far top left *Scrutineering may well be more formal than at home, complete with a time control.* (Lodge.)

Far left *A lot of razzamatazz at the start.* (Holmes.)

Above left *Roadside servicing is often the norm.* (Kolczak.)

Right *Overseas marshals are usually very knowledgeable. Printing clock in use here.* (Lodge.)

This page *Overseas control procedure: (1) Rally cars wait outside the yellow board.* (Kolczak.) *(2) Co-drivers walk into the control and wait for their minute to arrive.* (Kolczak.) *(3) At the appropriate time, co-driver summons driver and car into the control.* (Kolczak.)

things as they would on a club event. On the continent marshals and timekeepers will definitely know the score as far as their duties are concerned, so don't expect to get away with minor (or major) irregularities as you might do at home. The only thing that may fool them is the fact that you're turning up in a right-hand-drive car and they will come to the wrong side to sign your time card.

Abroad, you will usually find that the procedure at a time control is as follows: Rally car stops outside control area, co-driver walks in, hangs around marshalling table checking the time, calls driver and car in at appropriate time, hands in time card, gets back into car. In the UK, the practice of the co-driver walking into the control tends not to happen, as the marshals will come to the car once within the time control area and give you the time you ask for. When you do it the continental way (you don't have to, if you're confident your watch matches the official clock), the only thing to look out for is attracting the driver's attention while he's parked outside the control. As I think I said earlier, he may be dozing, chatting with other drivers or gazing at a pretty female spectator just when you want him to drive into the control. Some co-drivers have a whistle to wake their man up, drag him back to reality and get him into the control before the minute goes. Perhaps a briefing on this method would help to keep his mind on the rallying during the event.

Other things to look out for? Well, the regulations will be in a foreign language, though usually the organizers will have an English version if you ask for it. For some reason, the (compulsory) French version is taken as the definitive text in case of discrepancy. In practice, you will find that most people abroad will speak some English, so you shouldn't have too much trouble making yourself understood.

Quite often, stages may not be arrowed at all, since the organizers will assume you know your way around from the recce. Nor will there be maximum or minimum times on the special stages. In some countries, the local maps will horrify you for their lack of detail and accuracy. Quite often the only decent maps will be military ones and understandably these

Below left *(4) When the minute is up, co-driver hands in the time card.* (Lodge.)

Below right *Time cards are smaller overseas. On the left, a time card for a road section only; on the right, for a road section incorporating a stage.*

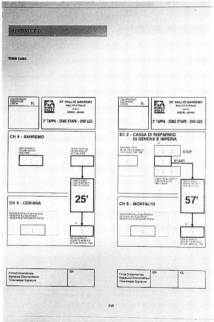

At the stop line, procedure is similar to the UK's. Note the board on the right for displaying individual stage times. (Lodge.)

will be virtually impossible to acquire. To help your service crew find their way, you might have to make some tulip diagrams, or redraw the map while on the recce. Some organizers produce excellent maps of the rally route and stages, making your service planning work easier. Generally, close to home and in 'civilized' countries you will find adequate maps commercially available, though sometimes these take a bit of unearthing. Here in Britain, I think the Ordnance Survey supplies are excellent.

Success

There's certainly no reason why you can't do well on your foreign events. British crews usually give a good account of themselves, perhaps because they're adaptable and respond to a challenge. The locals may have the benefit of local knowledge but apart from their very top crews, there are 'names' you may have read about which can certainly be beaten, whether it's for an overall placing or within the group or class. If you do put in a good performance, you can expect a very enthusiastic reception on the finish ramp and at the prizegiving. Who knows, you might pick up a reasonable bit of prize money as well, because the sponsorship and promotion of these events gives the organizers a bigger 'kitty' than our British events seem to find. Some events have a separate prize fund for foreign crews. Don't forget about the trade bonuses for which you may be eligible on an International event. If there are no British press on the event, ring up the magazines as soon as possible with your result—they'll be pleased to hear from you.

Further afield

Such is the attraction of rallying in, for instance, Belgium, that several British crews prefer to tackle rallies there than on the home championships. Given a few good results, better knowledge of the events and the experience to put deals together, it can be no more expensive and provide a lot of fun and experience for the whole team.

However, there are tougher challenges to be found beyond our shores. If it's fast, flowing gravel you're looking for, try the 1000 Lakes, but watch those jumps. If your driver wants to develop his snow driving technique (and there are few better ways of improving his car control than this), try Sweden or Finland in winter. For Alpine tarmac, there are some great rallies in Italy and France, including the famous Monte Carlo.

Monte Carlo

The only motoring event some non-enthusiasts have ever heard of is the Monte Carlo Rally. Today, this is not the great challenge of the past, though it's important to car manufacturers for image and publicity purposes. To do it seriously is very expensive, for you need a vast array of tyres from full studded snow to pure tarmac slick, as well as the service vehicles to carry that amount of rubber. With such a choice,

Below left *Studs or slicks? The unique gamble that is the Monte Carlo Rally.* (Kolczak.)

Below right *When driving on icy roads with racing tyres, a rally crew relies heavily on their ice note crews. Here, Francois Delecour's Ford waits with its slicks in the warmers, but clearly there is snow and ice about.* (Lodge.)

the difficulty facing the driver is to make a decision on tyre choice, so another essential for the serious competitor is an ice note crew, or rather three, to cover all the stages and get back to the service points with the information. This information allows the driver to make his tyre decision and provides the co-driver with specific locations within his notes of snow, ice, frost, gravel, water, etc. This is normally done by underlining in various colours, hence my recommendation not to use underlining for other indications in your pace notes. You also have to learn to read out this information in addition to your normal terminology. If the rally car is on pure slicks, your driver will certainly need to know about a patch of ice just in the braking area after a long straight, for example. There are also problems of spectators throwing snow into the road for 'fun'. In these circumstances, you will spend parts of stages on the wrong tyres, so your driver needs to learn about controlling the car, and himself, under these circumstances.

Monte Carlo is rather special and it's a pity that so few British crews venture forth to do it. I'm sure that by trimming the costs, it could be done reasonably well and provide a good result. There is a very well funded 'promotion' category for private entrants. Even if you don't get the chance to compete on Monte, you may be able to make ice notes for someone, which is great experience and gives you the chance to see other crews' notes in action. The technique of ice noting can be carried over to other events (when the ice note crew becomes the gravel note crew) because, as tyre choice is ever more critical, so the need for accurate, recent surface information becomes of prime importance.

Rougher events

If rougher gravel is the preference, try Spain, Portugal (with its slightly odd road book distance method), Greece or Cyprus. The latter is a particularly tough but enjoyable challenge, for which the organizers offer generous terms of support, though it's a long way from home. Clearly, if you're going to go for this sort of rally, you will need a strong, well prepared car, good service back-up and lots of tyres. However, such can be the rate of attrition that you can pick up a really good result with a sensible drive.

Some crews prefer still more adventure, in which case you could try some of the Middle East rallies, which use deserts for the stages, or even an African event. If the East African Safari seems a bit beyond you, you could always try the Ivory Coast, which, although WCR status, seldom attracts much in the way of works entries these days, so a privateer with a good strong car could get a very good result and have a great adventure into the bargain. You could go further afield still, and try the events in Argentina, Australia, Malaysia or New Zealand, all good rallies. Sometimes a good result on one of these will do you far more good than a whole season of British rallying. You'll broaden your rally experience considerably, as well as attract the attention of the bigger teams by a good performance. Obviously, costs are going to be high on these faraway rallies. It can be cheaper to rent a rally car from a team already committed to doing the rally for another customer, than to take your own car.

If you and your driver do wish to move up the rallying ladder, then your ability to do that may well be determined more by your drives abroad than in the UK. A 'home' result, however good, is looked on with some scepticism; a good 'away' result, even if against thinner opposition, will be taken as evidence of greater spirit and ability than merely thrashing round our British forests. Whatever your ambitions, the fact is that there is a lot of enjoyment and good experience attached to going overseas, so why not give it a try?

Chapter 13

Co-driving psychology

Up to now, we've looked mainly at the practical aspects of co-driving—how to do the work, how to sort the car, how to organize the team, how to move up the events ladder, and so on. Certainly, there are a lot of points to cover if you're going to do your job properly. But to some extent, that's only part of the co-driving game, because the mental aspects are just as important. You have to develop a mental rapport with your driver; that is a prime requisite. I'm not suggesting that you share the same personal interests, or even have the same attitude to things; in all probability, this will not be the case, but when you're on a rally together you should be joined by a common bond—a sense of purpose that has both of you concentrating on the same objective. To be able to do that, you must both trust each other.

Trust in the driver

A rally car is not an environment conducive to good relations. It's noisy, harsh and not built with comfortable motoring in mind. However well the pair of you have tailored it to your own requirements, you are to some extent captives of this vehicle, with all its irritations, in a situation of some pressure for most of the time. Pressure can have strange effects on people and even the best of friends can quarrel in the cauldron of competition. So in the first place there has to be trust. You must trust the driver, that he's going to do a good job at the wheel but not be so reckless as to constantly frighten you. Of course, there are bound to be times when you are alarmed or shaken by what occasionally happens on a special stage. If you don't get the odd worrying moment, then perhaps he's not going fast enough. What we're talking about here is real fear, because if you are constantly afraid of crashing, feeling that it might

206

happen at every corner, then you've no faith in your driver and you cannot do your job properly, however brave you are. If you find you are getting unsettled over this, it would help to discuss it with him rather than 'bottle it up'. He may accuse you of being an 'old woman', but it's to his advantage to get the joint act right, so that you can both give of your best.

Going off

If your driver is going off the road a lot, you have to decide if there's something wrong with his technique or attitude, or whether you can do something to calm him down. I used to hate going off the road. No-one enjoys such incidents at the time (though you may have a good laugh about them later), but what I disliked most about going off was not the possible harm I might come to—that's an acceptable risk—but the time lost and the possible detriment to the result. Crashes are dramatic, newsworthy items, but you shouldn't cultivate them as a habit just for that reason. Learn to hate 'offs' much as you should learn to hate all failure.

Trust in the co-driver

The driver too must have trust, in his co-driver. He must feel that you're competent, doing a good job for him and the team, and that you've got a good grip of the events. As you become more experienced you should be performing properly on the maps and pace notes, as well as looking after the thousand and one other tasks. By doing your homework before the rallies you should be on top of the events and this in turn gives the driver confidence in you and consequently in himself and the team. If he's not happy with you, he may say so directly, or his displeasure may manifest itself in more subtle ways. Whatever, it does you good to have a frank discussion about such problems, as it clears the air and may well resolve whatever difficulty exists.

The relationship

When I started rallying with John Taylor, he'd progressed from rallycross (in which there are no co-drivers) to rallying and seemed to have some difficulty in actually accepting that he had a co-driver to relate to. Initially, I think he had a fairly low opinion of co-drivers, but once he saw that I knew what I was doing, he was prepared to listen and to recognize that I could do quite a lot to help him. John will surely accept that he can be

The fruits of a good working relationship. Here David Llewellin sprays the champagne, while the author inspects the vintage before considering whether to follow suit. Victory on the Cartel Rally 1989. (Lodge.)

a rather abrasive character, and we did have our disagreements (I once got out of the car and walked off), but we developed the relationship and went on to achieve rather more success than many people expected.

These things are rather harder with a one-off 'ride'. I was once called in to co-drive for World Champion Walter Rohrl for the RAC Rally. Now Walter is no fan of the RAC Rally and turned up only the night before the start, which gave me little time to brief him properly or to establish a rapport for the event. We went off the road, rather a long way, I'm afraid. I always felt that if we'd had more time together before the rally, we could have sorted out a few things and maybe made a better attempt. You both need that common purpose I spoke of earlier.

Turning to another of my drivers, David Llewellin, there you have an example of a good working relationship. In terms of personality, we could hardly be more different. Our interests differed widely and we lived a long way from each other, yet once we were on a rally together we could concentrate on giving our very best, without any external influences to disrupt the relationship. Because we didn't see that much of each other between rallies, each meeting would be a fresh occasion when we would swop news and stories rather than becoming stale and bored. Particularly on a big programme, you spend a lot of time together on rallies, so it's not a bad idea to be apart when you're not rallying. Sometimes too much proximity can be a disruptive influence. Ours was a long-surviving partner-ship, because primarily the basis was right. He respected my experience and knowledge, I respected his driving and natural talent. Even so, there were times when we didn't always get along so well; there were occasions when both of us con-sidered taking another partner. But we stuck together and won a lot of rallies, including two RAC Open Championships. A good rally partnership has a lot of similarities to a marriage: you have your problems, but if you work at it, the relationship should flourish.

Difficult drivers

Not all drivers appreciate their co-drivers. To such drivers, co-drivers are just an added complication, some extra weight in the car, something the rules say they've got to have. That's a pity, because if they have that attitude they're not going to get the best from the co-driver. In this situation, the co-driver will be defensive, perhaps worrying too much about not making a mistake, rather than making a more positive contribution. Some drivers even regard the co-driver as competition, one of the opposition, whom they must beat into submission. This too is counter-productive. Perhaps they see him as a threat to their authority, because they don't necessarily relish having someone tell them what to do. For some, rally driving is a bit of an ego trip, so to be seen to be reliant on a co-driver is rather diminishing, in their minds. Drivers can be very strange crea-tures and I don't pretend to be a psychologist, or capable of unravelling all their little hang-ups. You have to sort each problem of the relationship yourself, for each situation is different.

The main thing in this state of affairs is not to be overawed. Stand your ground and don't let him grind you down. If you show strength of character, that there's a limit to what you'll take, he will come to accept that—or get a new co-driver. Perhaps mentally, he's not ideally suited to rallying, which is after all a 'team game'. But he'll respect you much less if you let him have his own way against your better judgement and allow him to walk all over you. The aim should be to achieve a balance in your relationship. It's no good the driver being totally dominant, because that crushes the spirit of the co-driver. Nor is it good for the co-driver to be totally dominant, because that will inhibit the flair of the driver. When I was with David Llewellin in his early professional years, I tried particu-larly hard not to 'rein him in' too much, because I reasoned that would stifle his natural talent. By giving him a 'freer rein', I knew we would end up off the road a few times, but at least he could learn his limits and express his natural ability in terms of speed. I felt he would be a winner sooner that way than if I attempted to subdue him, which as the 'senior professional' I was in a position to do.

Controlling the pace

I was first put in a car with David by Audi Sport UK, with the strict instructions not to allow him to crash. Now that's not always possible—if a driver's going to crash, then sometime or other he'll crash, co-driver notwithstanding. In the beginning our relationship was rather schoolmaster/pupil: he was the inexperienced tyro, just out of National rallying, I was the established pro. At rally forums, David often relates how I would judge the pace: 'Tidy it up' meant we were going quite well enough, thank you; 'Steady' meant we were about to go off; 'Jesus' meant we'd gone off but got away with it; 'Oh, David' meant we were on our roof or off the road for good. Slightly apocryphal, but you get the gist. It does no harm to have the driver recognize when you're becoming concerned. He may not realize, in the heat of the moment, that he's getting a bit ragged and over-confident. Your cooling words may well have the right effect. Sometimes the situation on the event or championship may dictate a more circumspect approach. It would be silly to lose the result for a bit of late-event showing off and probably the co-driver would be criticized for allowing that to happen. On the other hand, if you slow the driver down too much, he may lose concentration and make a mistake. It's a fine line between too fast and too slow, but you (and he) have to learn it.

There are times when the driver needs encouraging, perhaps after some sort of incident. On the Scottish one year with Malcolm Wilson, we brushed a tree, breaking his door window. His driving was a bit hesitant after that, until I punched him on the leg and said, 'Let's go' (or perhaps stronger words to that effect), whereupon he fired up again. It's really a question of developing a feel for the right pace; instinctively you as co-driver should know when your driver's not going well enough, and when he's trying too hard. Don't be afraid to speak out in either circumstance.

Media matters

Sometimes, speaking out is not always the best way to handle the media. As you become more proficient as a crew, you will become more prominent as personalities and the press will seek you out for views on proceedings. Generally, they will speak to the driver first, but they may look for the co-driver's view on a particular aspect of the rally. Now, a good co-driver usually plays his cards pretty close to his chest, so coming forth with an opinion may go against the grain. In fact, while the journalist may be looking for a 'punch-line' from the driver, he will probably expect a more balanced, factual account from the co-driver. You may be asked about a problem or incident that you have encountered. Depending on the situation, you must be careful not to say something that will criticize the driver too forthrightly, or the mechanics, the team management, the car, the tyres or the equipment, otherwise you run the risk of upsetting some important relationships. That doesn't leave you much room for manoeuvre, but in time you will learn to walk this particular tightrope and on occasion to be 'economical with the truth'. You could easily talk yourself out of a job, particularly higher up the rallying ladder. On the other hand, never tell actual lies. The press has a habit of finding out the truth during, or even after, a rally. If you have lied, you can hardly expect fair treatment in the future. 'No comment', or a referral to your team manager or other spokesperson is better than an outright lie. By all means be pleasant and courteous, but when you reach the 'grey areas' try to be diplomatic with your replies. Sometimes an amusing aside will get you out of a difficult situation.

Below left *Sometimes an amusing aside will get you out of an awkward situation in an interview. Ari Vatanen. (Kolczak.)*

Below right *The media may want to interview you at any time. Markku Alen, master of the clipped but entertaining response. (Kolczak.)*

Interviews

When you get to do bigger events, you may well be interviewed by a commentator, by a radio or TV interviewer, at scrutineering, at the start, during the rally, at the finish and, if successful, in the rally press office and at the prizegiving. There is a technique to being interviewed. The prime rule is to keep your answers short. No matter how difficult the question and how complex the answer ought to be, the audience don't really want to listen to a long, involved answer. Brief, though not monosyllabic, answers with plenty of expression go down the best, particularly if you can add a bit of humour, where appropriate, or make an interesting observation. You can develop the cult of the personality; people in high places will be looking for that. Being able to drive and co-drive is one thing; if you can communicate well and show a bit of character in front of a camera or a microphone, that means almost as much to a sponsor or manufacturer. Sometimes you will be asked really foolish questions, to which you might be tempted to give cutting replies. However, even though the interviewer may seem stupid to you, he may well be asking on behalf of the masses of people who understand little or nothing about rallying, so your answer should take that into account. Don't put him down too firmly, because that will make you seem patronizing to the audience.

Problem press

On occasions, the press and media can be rather unfair in making excessive demands on a crew's time. Promotional work and talking to the media is part of the job, but these people don't own you and should let you and your team get on with your work. A regular occurrence is for them to get in the way of the mechanics at work, but I recall that during our Open Championship years, the TV and press reporters would barely let David Llewellin have any peace at some service/ rest halts. He was very good and tolerant of this, but sometimes the 'reptiles' just go on expecting ever more and more, taking advantage of a driver's willingness to please. Try to steer him clear as diplomatically as possible; remember, the prime job is to win the rally, or whatever. The media come after that objective. A good working relationship with the press is, however, to everyone's advantage. They have a job to do, as much as yourself. Don't be afraid to ask them to leave you alone if you are under stress or if time is short. They will appreciate it if you can find time for them later in

Above left *Sometimes the media get in the way at service points, while the mechanics are trying to do their job.* (Kolczak.)

Above right *You may be required to attend a press conference or rally forum.* (Lodge.)

you can find time for them later in the event to answer, within reason, some of the questions you had to duck at the time.

There will be times when your words are misreported, misinterpreted or just plain falsified by a reporter, which can lead to friction. Some journalists have a nasty habit of twisting words to suit a particular 'angle' they are pursuing and have little compunction about 'dropping you in it', if that suits their purpose or the story they are trying to create. You will soon get to know these people, either by reputation or by bitter experience; you should therefore choose your words to them with particular care and if possible avoid discussion with them altogether.

Promotional work

If you've got yourself a sponsor or manufacturer's support, then the time will come for you to repay some of the debt you owe them. That could come in the form of a press conference or rally forum, at which you could be asked all sorts of interesting and impromptu questions. These events depend very much on the atmosphere; to a great extent, the audience make the running. If they're a bit flat, the forum doesn't come alive, but if you get a few lively questions, it can spark up quite nicely. Remember again to keep your answers reasonably short and to the point; if possible inject a bit of humour. A good chairman can make all the difference.

Dealer evenings

You could be attending a reception at a car dealership or other retail outlet, with the rally car on display and perhaps with rally films or videos for the audience. Again, you will find yourself answering questions, but on a more informal basis, quite often from young enthusiasts. These are the possible David Llewellins and Louise Aitken-Walkers of the future; the impression you give may well have a lasting effect, so make your answers simple but unpatronizing. Don't shrink from explaining the technicalities of the car or why things are done in a particular way. If asked to sign your autograph, do try to make it reasonably legible.

Dinner-dances

At some time you may be asked to speak at a motor club dinner-dance. Very few competitors actually relish this situation, but we've all had to do our stint. I tend to have a fairly standard speech, with a few tales of rallies and drivers gone by, which I vary according to the situation. By all means be entertaining, but remember that you may well have a mixed or even a youthful audience, so keep it reasonably presentable. As well as trying to keep the speech light and amusing, I usually like to include a serious note on rallying, but the tone is up to you and the situation as you see it. Even if you do not enjoy such occasions, the motor clubs do appreciate your

Always be prepared to spend time with younger enthusiasts. Christina Thorner, 1000 Lakes Rally, 1991. (Kolczak.)

Above left *The in-car camera is now a regular companion...* (Kolczak.)

Above right *...but the kit that goes with it can be appallingly cumbersome and fiddly to operate.* (Kolczak.)

presence. Don't forget it's their members who make your sport possible. The next time you meet those members could be when you're stuck in a muddy ditch and need their efforts to get you going again.

Mostly, drivers are the prime target for promotional activities, but I feel that co-drivers usually underplay their promotional value, being in general shy, retiring types. Well, some are! But you do have a part to play and particularly with the advent of the in-car camera, the role and contribution of the co-driver is being appreciated much more. Even though your driver may seem to have most of the limelight, there's no reason why you can't carve your own particular niche and create your own identity. You will be respected for that, as well as improve your prospects for professional employment. Always, when attending any sort of official function connected with rallying, do turn up looking smart. You may feel this is being over-conventional, but you are on show, in front of present sponsors and potential future sponsors. The near-standard 'blazer and greys' makes a much better impression than a pair of tatty jeans and a baggy sweater.

In-car camera

A few years ago the camera in the rally car was a revolutionary idea, but nowadays quite a lot of cars carry them. It all helps to get over to the public what rallying is all about. I must admit, I wasn't too fond of having the camera on board: the equipment wasn't too fond of having the camera on board: the equipment was bulky and heavy, it was an added complication (for me) to operate, I felt it intruded into the previously private driver/co-driver world (and disclosed some of our trade secrets) and for a long time seemed to bring a jinx with it. In time we got rid of the jinx and the installation improved, but I must admit I was always conscious of that 'eye' looking over my shoulder.

Going professional

To be honest, I never set out to become a professional co-driver. Indeed, I wasn't aware that you could even make a living at this activity until quite late. Nowadays, however, there are more opportunities, but it needs careful thought before taking the plunge. You might jump at the chance of a paid 'ride', but consider first the consequences. Rallying is a pretty volatile sport, dependent on the whims of sponsors and manufacturers. Rarely are contracts, particularly for co-drivers, for more than one year. So you never quite know what you're doing from one year to the next. If job security is important to you, perhaps because you have home commitments, then professional co-driving is not the best way to achieve that. What could be a good deal one year can fade away to nothing the following year, through no fault of your own. Your level of remuneration will be reasonable, but not anything like that of the driver. Perhaps that's unfair, because you will work just as hard, if not harder, and be at just as much risk as the driver, but that's the way it is. Only at World Championship level can you expect to make really substantial earnings as a co-driver.

Only very rarely does a team sign a co-driver and then start looking for a driver for him. So before you can make your contract, the driver has to conclude his. The 'silly season' as it is known can be a nerve-wracking time for a co-driver who is dependent on the sport for his living, for he is well down the order of priorities for sorting out. The driver may be looking for a change, the team manager might want someone else, the whole deal may depend on sponsorship which is agonizingly slow in coming through. So generally, September, October and November are not enjoyable months as the game of musical chairs is played for the following year; you just hope you can get your backside on the seat before the music stops.

Let me say that I never regretted becoming a professional co-driver for one moment. Yes, there were periods of uncertainty, but somehow, I always had confidence in my ability to find work within the sport. In my formative years I was fortunate to run a small business of my own which allowed me to take brief periods away at will. That meant I almost never had to turn down a 'ride', which increased my opportunities and experience quite rapidly. When my rallying reached a professional level, I was able to sell my small business and depend on co-driving full time. To be honest, this was rather daunting because, devoid of the security of my business, I took on far too much in my first full year as a pro, expecting to struggle to make ends meet. I had one contract for Internationals, another for Nationals, I did team management work at WCR level for another manufacturer and the odd rally freelance, while I also made the road book for the RAC Rally, co-ordinated a single-make championship and wrote a column for a monthly magazine in my spare time. In truth it was far too much, and though I acquitted myself well enough (I feel) on all fronts, I had to rationalize my work for the following year. That's just my own experience; other co-drivers have different tales to tell as to how they became professional. There is a certain amount of luck involved—being in the right place at the right time and so on. But your own particular circumstances will have quite a bearing on the issue.

If you're lucky enough to be offered a professional co-driving contract, you'll probably take it, but do weigh up all the pros and cons—it's not all plain sailing, by any means. If you have some other source of income, whether it's a business or profession of your own, or something within the sport like some co-ordinating or PR work or journalism, it gives you that bit of extra security and reduces the possibility of the unscrupulous taking advantage of your sole dependence on co-driving.

Team managers

Once you get into the realms of professional rallying, you will have to deal with a team manager. Whereas in the past your allegiance rested solely with the driver, you now have two loyalties—one to your driver and one to the man who pays you. That shouldn't be a conflict but occasionally it can be. The team manager will expect you to do things his, or the team's, way—not unreasonably. That might not be the driver's way and you must be careful that you don't become a bit of a football between the two. If a driver isn't happy with a situation in the team, but doesn't want to be the one to express disfavour, he may well create a situation that causes the co-driver to generate the complaint. So the co-driver is made to seem the trouble-maker, while the driver stands apart from the situation. Clever. Or it might work the other way; the team manager

Left *At professional level you will need to work with your team manager. Ove Andersson and Bjorn Waldegaard discuss the state of affairs on the 1990 Safari Rally.* (Selden.)

Below *Special promotional events make good TV, but don't require co-drivers and aren't proper rallies.* (Kolczak.)

might wish to impart some bad news to the driver, but doesn't wish to upset his 'star' by telling him directly. The co-driver, appraised of the bad news by the manager, may attract the disfavour of the driver, or at least take the heat off the boss. I wrote earlier about 'don't shoot the messenger'—well, it's a similar situation. You need a broad back and the mentality of a diplomat to survive as a co-driver in some teams. But to be fair, I had very few problems with team managers. Perhaps I was lucky.

The future

There has never been such a high level of interest in World Championship level rallying as there is today. This has had the effect of diminishing the relevance of other series, such as the European Championship and our own British Open Championship, which during the '70s and '80s enjoyed a status almost on a par with the World series. The pre-eminence of the World Championship has brought about more involvement by manu-

facturers, which has increased the opportunities for drivers and co-drivers. These things go in cycles and depend on outside influences well beyond our control, such as the world trade in motor cars, the price of fuel, safety and environmental issues. In the short term, the outlook seems good, but these things can change quite rapidly. For British co-drivers, it's a good situation that we have many World Championship teams based in the UK, for this presents several opportunities, either to work as co-drivers or on the team management/co-ordination side of things. I think it's no coincidence that the majority of World Championship teams are presently co-ordinated by former top British co-drivers.

Looking longer term, we have to try to see where co-driving is going, and we also have to examine where rallying is going. Undoubtedly the sport will suffer more restrictions in certain parts of Europe as the availability of terrain is reduced by environmental pressures and local lobbies against such activities. The sport has always been expensive, but to succeed at the very top level demands such a strong financial commitment that only a very few teams are able to afford full involvement. Somehow, the governing body has to bring the costs down, either by reducing the number of events or the sheer technical expense, otherwise rallying runs the risk of pricing itself out of existence.

If in Europe the events are likely to be diminished, there are other parts of the world where rallying should grow. The Middle East, Africa, South and North America and Australasia all have the terrain to accommodate rallying and perhaps offer a greater challenge. To some extent, the challenge of the European events is being steadily diluted. For rallying to be credible as a promotional activity, as well as a technical exercise, there has to be a challenge, which is perhaps why events like Paris–Dakar have captured the public imagination. The man in the street can grasp the enormity of such a drive, whereas anybody can drive to Monte Carlo these days, can't they?

There is also a tendency towards special promotional 'rallies', such as the Race of Champions, Bettega Memorial and special TV Challenges. These may make good TV, but they're not true rallying and significantly several of these events do not feature co-drivers, as there is no requirement to navigate or timekeep within the car. Undoubtedly, technology exists which is capable of replacing the co-driver by a computerized machine and a 'head-up' display on the windscreen, but there is neither the demand nor the wherewithal to bring this about. In any case, this would require a serious rule change by FISA and I cannot detect any pressure for such a change at present.

Just think of the mix-ups drivers could get themselves into without a co-driver on board.

If rallying changes substantially, aiming to 'package' the sport for television, then the co-driver's existence is at risk. Yet if it doesn't change in terms of costs or environmental acceptability, the whole sport is at risk. Somewhere in between there must be a balance which will maintain the challenge of the sport, yet keep it in touch with public opinion and realistic costs for participants, be it at World Championship or Club level. Traditionally, rallying has been all about putting a near-standard motor car and its two-man crew through a rigorous challenge. That's the way it should always be. So long as the sport continues in this direction, there will always be a place for co-drivers.

Index